ROZA'S WAR
Diary of a Soviet Sniper
Brenda Muller Ellis

©2024 Brenda Muller Ellis. All rights reserved. No part of this publication may be reproduced or used in any form or by any means, graphic, electronic or mechanical, including photocopying, recording, taping, or information and retrieval systems without written permission of the publisher. This is a work of fiction. Names, characters, and incidents either are the product of the author's imagination or are used fictitiously. Any resemblance to real persons, living or dead, is purely coincidental.

Published by Hellgate Press
(An imprint of L&R Publishing, LLC)
2305 Ashland St., #104-176
Ashland, OR 97520
email: sales@hellgatepress.com

Book design: Michael Campbell
Cover design: L. Redding

Author photo by Chloe Ellis

ISBN: 978-1-954163-94-2

Library of Congress Catalog-In-Data information available upon request

Printed and bound in the United States of America First edition 10 9 8 7 6 5 4 3 2 1

ROZA'S WAR

Diary of a Soviet Sniper

BRENDA MULLER ELLIS

CONTENTS

Introduction . . . . *vii*

First Journal: Spring *1*

Second Journal: Summer *49*

Third Journal: Autumn *121*

Fourth Journal: Winter *165*

Afterword *213*

A Note from the Author *217*

About the Author *237*

Bibliography *239*

INTRODUCTION

ROZA SHANINA was a member of the first generation of the Soviet experiment, born in 1924 in central Ukraine, where her father, Yegor Shanin, a Bolshevik Party Director, ran the *Bogdanovka* collective farm. The family left the area in 1932, during the height of the *Holodomor* (a man-made famine that decimated Ukraine,) possibly due to a need to escape the peasant uprisings against the increasingly brutal collectivization policies of the Communists. The Shanins moved to the village of Yedma, Arkhangelsk Oblast, Northern Russia, and settled there permanently, with Yegor Shanin serving as Party Director in charge of several collective farms. At age fourteen, Roza ran away from their home in Yedma after a fight with her father, and went to live her brother, Fyodor, in the city of Arkhangelsk, where she applied and was accepted into secondary school.

Three years later, in 1941, the Nazis invaded the Soviet Union, taking the citizens and Stalin by complete surprise, so much so that Stalin refused to believe it. He and Hitler had a pact, an understanding, and mutual respect and esteem. Why would Hitler betray him, Josef Stalin? They agreed in every particular.

But Hitler never liked Stalin, called him a "sub-human ape" behind his back, and when the time was right, ordered his prized *Einsatzgruppen* "murder squads" to burn every village, rape every woman, leave no Slav alive on their warpath from Germany to the Kremlin in Moscow. The people and towns of Poland and Lithuania were decimated with sadistic zeal, but Stalin couldn't face the truth until it was too late to mount a real defense. When he finally woke up, Stalin pulled his troops out of Finland and sent them to beat back the Germans. But this was a small, weak Red Army, no more than an annoying fly to Germany's elite *Wehrmacht*, who swatted it away with ease.

Now Stalin had a real problem. Hitler was after him, and what could he do, with no real army? Three years earlier, during the Great Purge of 1938, a paranoid Stalin had executed nearly all of his officers and commanders to stamp out the possibility of a military coup, and in 1941, he had few soldiers and almost no one with any military experience to lead them. Stalin issued a widespread draft, put his yes-men in positions of command, and sent everyone off to defend the Motherland. They were annihilated—millions of young Soviet boys died—including Mikhail and Fyodor Shanin, two of Roza Shanina's older brothers.

Roza's life changed dramatically after the war began. Fyodor, her brother/protector in Arkhangelsk, was conscripted almost immediately into the Red Army, and Roza was on her own. Before the war, secondary school had been free, and students received a stipend and a dormitory room to live in. During the war, tuition was charged, student stipends were canceled and dormitory rooms were too expensive to be practical. Roza was forced to leave school and find work to pay for room and board. She was fortunate to get hired as a school teacher at the Kindergarten #2 in Arkhangelsk. The job came with a small apartment attached to the Kindergarten, and Roza used her almost all of modest income to pay tuition so she could continue her education.

When Roza's supervisor at the Kindergarten #2, Anna Tamarova, found her passed out from hunger and exhaustion in the little office behind her classroom (wearing her only dress, which was gray, made of paper,) she went to some trouble to make sure Roza's position was secure, and got permission for her to eat with the students in the school cafeteria. With these arrangements, Roza was able to survive the first years of the war, finish secondary school and one year at university, and get some real clothes.

Acts of kindness, such as that of Anna Tamarova, happened often during this time. The normal dangers and fears of Soviet life were displaced by the war—everything was *For the Front!* Citizens found themselves able to look out for one another without fear of standing out, of being labeled an *Enemy of the People*. The whisperers went quiet, and unity was the thing, a new and beautiful thing, which created a patriotic zeal that helped to support the red fury that the Communist Party propagandized amongst the people. *Destroy the Enemy!* was the constant cry. *Crush the Fascist Beast!* Everyone was wild to join the fight, to put their lives on the line for their comrades. Here was meaning, here was purpose! The competition was stoked; who could give more, who was truly selfless?

When Roza heard of her brother Mikhail's death at Leningrad, followed by Fyodor's disappearance and probable death at Stalingrad, she was ready to go to the ends of the earth to avenge her brothers, to prove her worth. She spent a full year trying to enlist, reportedly banging down the doors of Red Army officers, but was turned down again and again. *No females allowed*, was the reply at first. Later, after the Red Army had lost almost an entire generation of young men, and began to accept females in their ranks, they decided that women were well suited to sniper work, due to their higher percentage of body fat and naturally patient dispositions. The Women's Central Sniper School was formed, and began enrolling Soviet females who were physically fit, had passed at least seven secondary school classes, and had gone through a four-day *Vsevobuch* basic training program. Roza applied and was accepted in June 1943.

Prior to boarding the train to the frontlines on April 2, 1944, Roza met her mother, sister, and younger brothers in Bereznik, a town near Yedma where her Aunt Agnes lived and where Roza had attended middle school. During this farewell visit, Roza was gifted a blank journal by her younger sister, Yulia. *Roza's War* is a fictional re-creation of that journal, built upon known facts about the real-life Roza Shanina's time at the Front during World War Two.

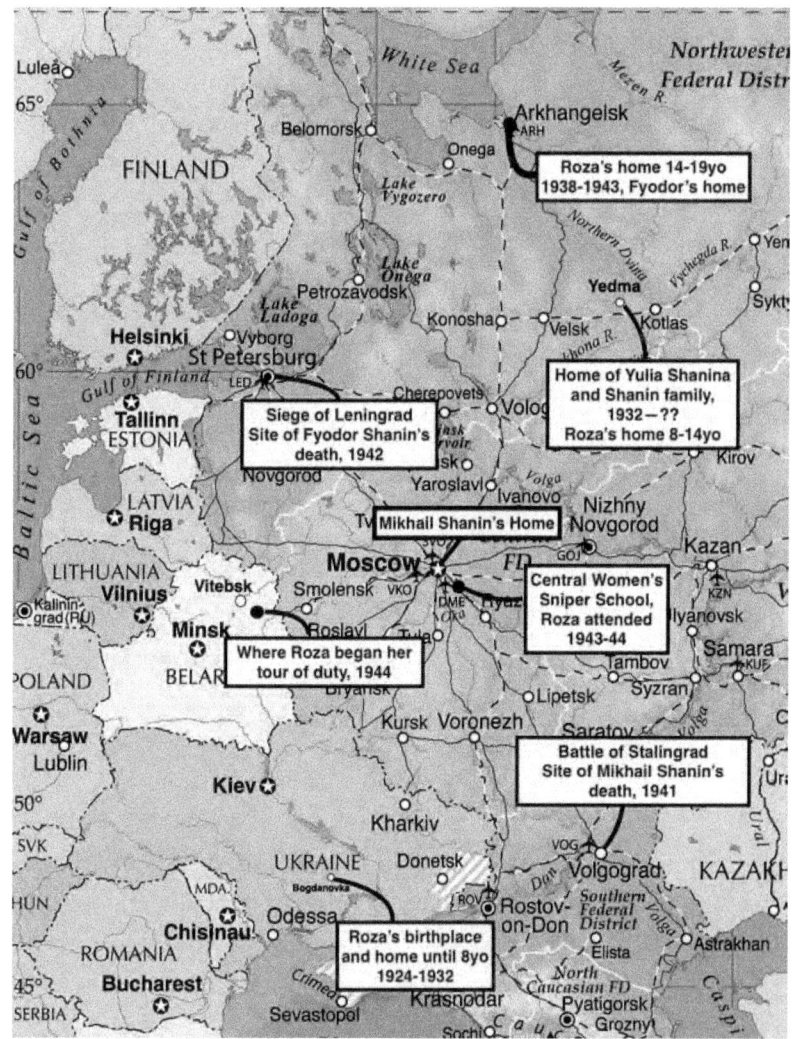

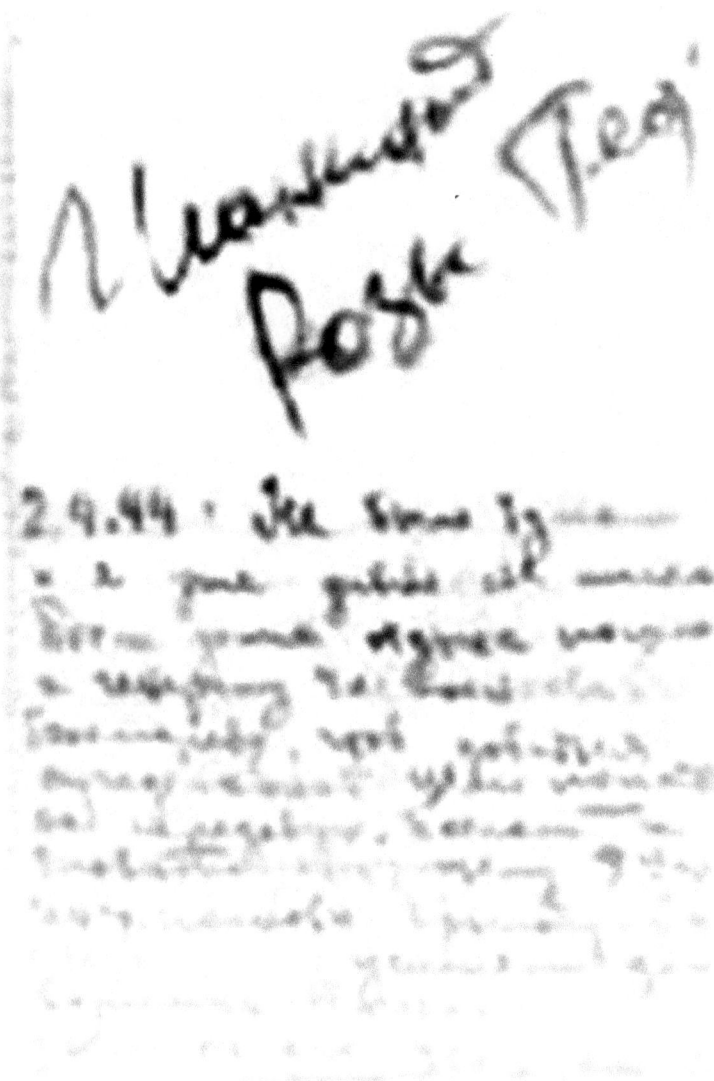

FIRST JOURNAL:
SPRING

2.Apr.44
On a train, somewhere between Moscow and Smolensk

Finally, the train has left the Moscow station. What a mash up! Six hundred girl snipers crowded onto the platform, set to be deployed, waiting and waiting in the soft rain, when a fat captain with red cheeks called us to attention, put his hands and his hips and hollered "Well girls, are you here to fight or to fuck?" Can you believe it? Then came the muttering — *What's the difference? What the devil?* and *Mudak*[1] — but I think the captain didn't catch on (thank the gods!) because he just kept preaching at us about how we mustn't act like *zenschinas*[2] when we get to the frontlines. We only escaped when a sergeant came to hand out papers.

Not an auspicious beginning, but I won't let it bring me down. Now, the train speeds toward the frontlines, toward my destiny as a sniper on the Western Front. I've been working toward this moment for so long, so many years of training and longing to distinguish myself, to fight against the evil creatures who have so insulted our people. I want to be a great and extraordinary warrior. My will is strong — I wish with a thousand wishes that my ability will meet my desire. I did well at sniper school, but war must be different, must have bigger challenges. And they've made me commander, although I've never been a boss. It seems like it would be better to give orders than follow them, I'm not at all sure. I don't like to tell people what to do, but I'll have to, in this job. Will I be good at it?

---

1   *Mudak:* Russian slang for jerk or asshole.
2   *Zenschina:* Russian for whore. Interestingly, there is no Russian word for woman – females are either *devotchkas* (girls), *babushkas* (grandmothers), or *zenschinas*.

But here is home, this journal in my hands, to soothe my nerves. Such a thoughtful gift, Yulia. You always understand me best. Oh, how I love to write! Putting things down on paper sets my thoughts in order like nothing else. Nothing can bother me too much, as long as I can write about it.

Next stop, Smolensk, and then we will be transported in some way into Belorussia, to Vitebsk, where I will be commander of the girls' sniper platoon of the 184th Rifle Division, Fifth Army, Western Front. And my new life will begin.

3.Apr.44
Sitting on my bunk, new platoon quarters

When I jumped off the train at Smolensk, a blue cap[3] was waiting for me on the platform. He approached, said "You are Roza Shanina?" and handed me a letter, which turned out to be from our brother Sergei. God and Hell, Yulia, such a letter! And why did he send it to me, of all people? I must be Sergei's least favorite sibling. But I guess I'm the only one in the army who is still alive. Maybe that makes me convenient.

Dear Roza,

This is the first letter I've written you. You think me a bad brother, and perhaps it's true. I've never been what Fyodor

---

3   SMERSH officers, commonly known as "blue caps," were security agents whose primary job was counter-intelligence for the Red Army, and routing out anti-Soviet elements in military and civilian populations.

was to you. I was blinded by Papa, always seeing you as he did, as the thorn in his side. Now the blindfold has been ripped off and I see that you were right all along, that I am the stupid one. Where have duty and loyalty gotten me? In prison, labeled a traitor.

Now I must kiss the dirt and beg a favor. I need you to bring this letter to Papa. You'll read it, to know what you carry, to know my situation, and that's fine. I'm sorry to burden you. Sorry for everything. I'm desperate. You must have some leave coming up. Do your big brother a favor and take your leave in Yedma.

Ostat'sya v zhivykh,[4]
Serge

19.March.44
Lubyanka prison,[5] Moscow

Dear Papa,

Trouble has found me and I write to beg your help. On the 18th of March, I was put on trial and convicted of three charges: abuse of power, failure to carry out orders, and misconduct in the presence of the enemy. This is some sort of terrible mistake, or else somebody wants me dead. They've

---

4   Russian for "stay alive."
5   The Lubyanka building in Moscow was the headquarters of the NKVD and contained a prison on the two uppermost floors that was used mostly for political prisoners.

thrown me into a prison cell in the Lubyanka and sentenced me to ten years hard labor. I requested a retrial, naturally, and I think it must have been allowed, because I'm still here in prison rather than on my way to Siberia, but how can I hope for a different outcome from the second trial if nothing changes?

You pushed me to the NKVD,[6] to this hard life that has made me fall so far from who I used to be. I've fought with myself to be a good worker, and I've served faithfully for two years. I've done some hard and terrible things, under their orders, and now they call me a traitor and invent charges against me. You have the ear of some powerful people in the Politburo. I beg your help to get me out of hard labor, or worse. If not for myself then for Maria, and for your new grandson, Alexei Sergeivich, who doesn't deserve to lose his father before he's learned to walk. I have nowhere else to turn.

*Your son,
Sergei*

Poor Sergei! But what does he think I can do about it? I just got here, how can I possibly take leave to deliver his letter? Probably, he's heard only that I enlisted and went to sniper school, and doesn't know that I've just been deployed. And yet, if a blue cap could get to Smolensk, he could surely get to Papa in Yedma. But the Party might be watching Papa.

---

6   The NKVD, or the People's Comissariat for Internal Affairs, was the precursor to the KGB, widely-known and feared for their brutal methods of repression. SMERSH was a branch of the NKVD.

I suppose it makes sense, but it's a lousy birthday present. I'll have to keep it hidden until I figure out what to do.

I'm twenty years old today. I don't expect any attention, but turning twenty hasn't been the milestone I always imagined it would be. More like gravel. No one here even knows to wish me cheer, but you'll think of me, Yulechka.

Stupid Sergei! How could he get himself thrown into prison? He, a blue cap! I expect he has done "hard and terrible things." How am I supposed to feel about that? Do I even want to help him?

Sorry. I know you love him so. He is my brother. I mustn't judge without more information. How I wish he hadn't sent that letter to me! Because now, if I don't get it to Papa before the retrial, I will share in the responsibility for Sergei's ruin, and maybe his death.

4.4.44, 21:17
Platoon billet

We saw our first action today, in the trenches along the south road that leads into Vitebsk. *Too fast!* some of the girls complained, wanting more time to settle into our new quarters, but you will know that it suited me fine. I was glad for the distraction.

The platoon is billeted to an old farmhouse east of Vitebsk. It's thin, has very little in it, but it's all ours. I have so much to tell you about this place, about all of the people I've met, but first I want to write about work.

Our orders today were to watch Vitebsk's south road, and shoot any Nazi officers who came along, ignoring the lower ranks as they aren't worth giving away our position. Last week, the 5th Army forced Fritz[7] to retreat from Smolensk back to Vitebsk, and now we are called in as part of the effort to make sure they don't push back.

We dropped into the trenches before sunrise, my trigger finger itchy to try out my new M44 Mosina. It's not brand new, but what a beauty! Five-shot, bolt-action, internal magazine, with a 3.5 PU fixed scope and a range up to 1000 m—the most powerful rifle I've ever held in my hands. We shot some Mosinas at sniper school, but they were the M38-40s with the old-style scopes. We also shot Berdans, but they're just single-shots, only good at close range. My new Mosina is a much finer piece of machinery, and it's all mine. Most of the snipers have names for their rifles—I'll need to think of a good one.

Do you remember how Papa described the trenches in the Great War? He said they were huge tunnels that made up a giant maze, with whole villages inside. Ours are nothing like that—there's only room for two or three snipers in a trench hole. Sometimes only one. Sometimes we dig shallow passages between the trenches, to make a long trench line, and today we were working in this kind of connected trench system.

Lida Vdovina, from sniper school, was my partner, and we stood in the mud for hours, watching and waiting. You would not like this work, Yulia, especially now, with the constant rains of the *raputitsa*[8] upon us. The trenches are mucky holes in the ground, like Aunt Agnes' pigsties but somehow so much worse because of the rats (who, like the pigs, eat anything that you leave lying around, and not just food,) and maybe also because we are trapped there and can't move around much at all. Lida set her ration on top of her rucksack for two seconds and we saw it snatched away out of

---

7   Nazis were commonly referred to as "Fritz" or "Fritzes" by the Soviets during WW2.

8   *Raputitsa:* the rainy season in Russia, also commonly used to describe the muddy, impassable roads of the rainy season.

the corner of our eyes, with a flash of something gray. For an hour after that, I couldn't shake the feeling that little beady eyes were constantly watching us. But it does no good to think about such things, and really it's a huge distraction from keeping watch on the road, so we put it out of our minds and took turns scanning the road for hours, for such a long time with nothing more interesting to look at than an occasional truck. It seemed a thousand hours passed like this, and I was becoming more and more certain that nothing would ever happen, when Lida said—"that Fritz?"

I jumped up and grabbed my binoculars to have a look, and saw a car speeding south from the city, the open-style car that German officers prefer, carrying two men. As they came closer, I saw that their uniforms were blue, and that one of them wore an officer's cap. How amazing, that he wore his rank so boldly!

I tracked him through the binoculars, saw his pale face, his strong nose and black goggles. Young, maybe my age, or not much older. I switched over to my M44 and peered through my scope with my heart in my ears, my senses tingling. The car wasn't going fast, with the extreme mud of the *raputitsa* roads, so I had plenty of time to calculate the deflective distance and set my sights parallel to the middle of his chest, like they trained us to do for moving targets at sniper school. I was on target—he was in range, the car was practically in front of us, it was time to fire, and I froze. I knew my orders, knew exactly what to do, but my body wouldn't obey.

Every person I knew, everything that has ever happened to me was yelling *Shoot!* in my head, and then I thought, *Why me?* Why was I the one to make this decision? But then, it wasn't really *my* decision, I was following orders. But orders don't pull triggers, Yulia, and in that moment I felt my power. A man's life would end with my action. Was I really going to kill someone?

I wondered about the man himself, whose life was in my crosshairs. Was he a loyal Nazi, or was he forced into service? Or maybe this was a Russian boy, forced to dress as a Nazi officer and drive by our trench. How could I tell the difference?

I could miss, or I could shoot to injure, and no one would know my intention. My aim is very good, Yulia. But I had to fire my rifle. I couldn't stand the judgment that would come from doing nothing. From nothing, I would be called Coward. If I shot and missed the kill, I'd be judged incompetent, and not just by others, but also by myself. I had to kill this man, or I would never do well as a sniper. I wouldn't be useful to my country, would never get any medals, never be a great and exceptional warrior. If I shot true, I might have all of those things, and I'd also be a killer.

These thoughts took over everything, like a screaming baby, and I couldn't focus. I needed to act, to take my shot, before the chance was lost.

Suddenly Fyodor was there, in a memory that pushed up to the surface. *Fascist beasts!* he cried, his face contorted. We'd been looking at a photograph in *Pravda*[9] just after the Germans invaded. A young Lithuanian girl hung from a tree, naked, blood smeared from between her legs all the way down to her feet, someone's home burning in the background. Fyodor had been so angry, so full of hate!

Remembering Fedya at that moment, and how he died at Leningrad, months later, all I could think was that I wanted someone to pay, Yulia. I was crying and I couldn't breathe past the ball in my throat, but I fired my weapon, and I knew my aim was true as soon as I squeezed the trigger. Through my scope, I saw the bullet tear into the Nazi's chest. I watched the torso slam back hard, the head snap over the bench, the body slide into stillness.

---

9   *Pravda* (the Russian word for "truth") was the widely-distributed official magazine of Soviet communism from 1918–1991. It was required reading for party members, used largely to spread propaganda.

And then I was giddy, almost euphoric, and everything turned sharp and bright. *I got him!* I thought, and felt the urge to leap out of the trench and chase down the car to see the dead body. It seemed that one jump would have sent me soaring twenty feet into the air, and I tensed, wanting that jump. But then every muscle in my body seemed to melt, and I slid down the side of the trench.

I've killed a man. I must have said this out loud, because suddenly Lida put her hand on my shoulder.

"You killed a fascist," she said. "Great shot!"

I needed to hear that, and I found a smile for Lida. The rest of the afternoon, I moved with a bit more zip, and *an eye for an eye* kept running through my mind. You know what that means—if someone gouges out someone's eye, they should be punished by losing their own eye. So this Nazi officer had it coming to him, because his people killed our big brother. But that specific guy didn't kill Fedya. Did he deserve to die? And if he did, do I deserve to die for killing him? If we follow that logic, who will be left who deserves to live!

Certainly, we know that life and death aren't fair. What is life? What is death? Why live? Live, until you die, comes the answer. Live, because we are here.

Later, I made a mark in my gray book and the girls congratulated me on opening my tally. After dinner, I went to bed with everyone else, early, so we can get to the trenches before the sun comes up tomorrow, and in the darkness, I started crying and couldn't stop. I wasn't sobbing, it was more like tears and sniffles that wouldn't stop coming. I was sure that my new bunkmates, Sasha Ekimova and Kaleriya Petrova, who I barely know, could hear everything and I was ashamed. But then Sasha was there, right next to my bunk, whispering to me.

"It's okay, Roza, cry as much as you want. It happens to everyone the first time. It gets easier."

"It does?" I asked, sounding like a small child.

"Much. I promise."

Then she climbed back into her bunk, and my shame was overcome by gratitude. I won't say the shame disappeared, but I felt so much better in knowing that someone cared enough to try to comfort me.

I can tell by their breathing that Sasha and Kali are both asleep now, but I've given up. Every time I close my eyes, I see the dead Nazi painted inside my eyelids, which is too scary for sleeping. Sitting on my bunk with my back against the wall, like last night, it occurs to me that I'm the same Roza that I was last night, the same Roza I've ever been, but now I'm a killer, and that's a strange idea, like I'm a little bit more evil, a little bit more powerful. I'm not sure how to think of myself. I keep imagining newspaper headlines.

SHARP SHOOTER ROZA SHANINA GUNS DOWN ENEMY OFFICER IN MOVING VEHICLE. ROZA SHANINA KILLS RUSSIAN BOY DISGUISED AS NAZI. KILLER ROZA SHANINA EXTERMINATES FELLOW HUMAN.

I hope killing a man doesn't make me a horrible person. I hope the rules are different for soldiers. I think they must be, Yulia. We must kill the enemy. What choice do we have, as soldiers? I'm relieved that I was able to go through with it, so I don't know where this confusion is coming from. Probably I'm just tired. Everything will be clear tomorrow.

5.4.44, 4:12

Dreamt of Fyodor, just now. I was alone in a room with no windows or doors, nothing at all except for a box made of rough wood, a big square box, big enough to hold something important, or nothing at all. I wondered if it held the man I shot, and looked at it, fearing it, and then I was inside the box, in total darkness, cramped, wood pressing into me all around, and it turned into a coffin. I couldn't move and I panicked, banging my head on the lid, calling for help, and then Fyodor was there, standing next to the box. I saw him from above, as if some part of me floated near the ceiling, while my body was still trapped in the coffin. He looked perfect, happy, smiling. I thought how handsome death had made him. My eyes took him in eagerly, until I saw the giant hole in his chest, and I understood that it was I who had shot him, I who had killed him, and I was horrified. *Fedya, forgive me*, I cried, but no sound came out. *Fyodor!* I screamed, still no sound. Then we were in the box together, and it wasn't small, we both fit fine. He wrapped himself around me, holding me, and my terror slid away, replaced by a feeling of total safety. I woke up just now. What do you think it means, Yulia? I want to believe that Fyodor is watching over me, that he didn't end with his death.

5.4.44, 22:12
On my bunk, sniper quarters

We had the day off today so not much action. It's been a long time since I've had a whole day without drills or orders. You'd think *hurrah!* but today seemed a week long, with far too much time to think about the Nazi I shot yesterday, and to re-examine Sergei's letter. I'm going to make myself mental wondering what on earth to do about that letter. I wandered around the woods all morning, brooding about how to get it to Papa, and came to the conclusion that I have no way of doing this. I'm determined to put it out of my mind, as much as I can, until I get leave or something else occurs to me.

There was a much better use of my day off—getting to know the other snipers and our camp, so I spent the rest of the day doing just that. You'd be amazed how many soldiers are here, how absolutely enormous this camp is. We have twelve girls in my platoon, which is attached to one of ten rifle divisions in the 5th Army, three tank brigades, an engineering division, seven artillery regiments, a support division, and more regiments that I've seen but don't know anything about. That's just our Army, and we're stationed here with several other armies, who have similar forces, all together making up the Western Front, around 300,000 soldiers. We are massive, like a big city on the Front, only with tents and tanks in place of buildings. Captain Pavel Blokhin is our battalion's commander. I haven't seen him yet, but I'm likely to meet him at some point.

Three other girls from my class at sniper school were assigned to our platoon, and we arrived together two days ago in a Willys[10] jeep, which is a small American truck with no roof. It was bit of a mash-up with the four of us and the driver, but we all liked it. The sun had just gone down when we pulled up to the rough wooden farmhouse that was billeted out to our platoon. We unloaded our gear onto the porch and poked around, exploring the front room and the small side rooms that were loaded up with pallet bunks, and waited for the rest of the snipers to get back from working the trenches.

The snipers trooped in shortly after dark, looked us over and nodded as they lined up their boots next to the door and stripped off their camouflage. When they learned that I was their new commander, their eyes stayed on me, waiting to see what I would say or do, as commander. I wanted to say just the right thing, but in

---

10   Created in 1940, the Willys remains the template for today's jeeps. The U.S. sent 52,000 Willys jeeps to the U.S.S.R. during WW2.

truth I was afraid to open my mouth, afraid I would come off too strong or too weak, so I just went around with the other girls and shook everyone's hand.

I like Sasha and Kali (Kaleriya) best, which is good news because the three of us share a bedroom. Really, it's an old servants' room with three pallet bunks built into one wall. I don't mind the close quarters at all. I much prefer to be in a small space with two other people than in the larger bedroom with six.

My impressions of Sasha and Kali after knowing them for three days. Sasha is friendly, with pretty blue eyes, seems determined to be cheerful, and likes to keep things orderly. She's a good shot, but I don't think she's driven to succeed — she's passing the time. But she shoots well when she does shoot. She keeps her uniform clean, with all of its buttons and straps in their right place. Kali is quieter, likes to stay in the background, and seems very intelligent. She has dark hair and eyes. I think she's from the east. I don't know her as well yet, because she doesn't talk as much as Sasha, who keeps up a running chatter a lot of the time. They are field partners and can usually be found next to each other. I'm drawn to them, in that mysterious way that sometimes happens, when you go sit next to someone and sit very close and stick with them and you have no idea why. I'm glad they had an open bunk in their room.

I don't know the other girls well, except the ones who came with me from sniper school, but I feel their eyes on me often, perhaps because I'm their commander. My authority, or higher pay grade, or something, marks me different. This is no problem for me — I'm no stranger to being different, being just a little outside the regular crowd. Such was our life growing up on the *kolkhoz*, was it not? With Papa around, everyone was always a little afraid of us.

7.4.44
Evening at the sniper house

Our billet is an old farmhouse, not so different from our old house. Not the house in Yedma, which is nicer, but the old house in Ukraine, which you might not remember because you were pretty young when we moved. This must have been someone's home before the war, but everything has been stripped down. We have a common room, the kitchen, and three rooms that serve as sleeping quarters. It's all very utilitarian — no art, no comfortable chairs in which to sit and read or waste time pondering War and Life and what we're doing here. The only furniture in the place is the big table where we eat breakfast, with two long, wooden benches on either side and a few ragtag chairs at the ends.

When we got back from the trenches tonight, I was surprised to see a man bent over a bowl of something at the far end of the table, a thin, frowning man. We'd been told "no men allowed" very clearly, there's even a sign on the door. "Who's that?" I asked. "One-and-a-half-Ivans," Sasha said, under her breath. I guess they call him that because he's so tall. He guards our platoon, and makes sure no one comes in or out after curfew.

My first reaction was to be pleased that the army had put some measures in place to protect us, given the general "are you here to fight or fuck" mentality of the officers, but Sasha laughed at that, and insisted he was there to guard us against ourselves, against our "base instincts" that would have us sleeping in a different soldier's bed every night.

"You don't have trouble sneaking out," Kali said to Sasha, and an argument broke out, with Sasha feeling accused and Kali hinting at some kind of moral superiority. It seems that Sasha has a serious boyfriend, and spends some nights with him, but Kali doesn't like it. I was surprised that they were arguing, they seem such good friends.

But it didn't make me too nervous, even with all of the guns in the room. It wasn't *that* kind of arguing, so I just stayed out of it until they calmed down. I really wanted to ask how Sasha could form a relationship with a boy out here, when he could be killed at any time, but I didn't have the nerve to ask. Instead, I asked if things were better for women now than they'd been at the start of the war. If we were safer, less likely to be attacked or harassed.

Turns out the situation is only slightly better. We have guards now, but the attitude is much the same — army women are loose, and if a woman resists, she doesn't really mean to. If a woman is taken by force, it's likely she'll be blamed for it.

"Carry a knife in your boot," Kali said darkly, and I will.

I feel a desperate kind of rage at hearing this, and almost welcome the idea of introducing my blade to a male aggressor. Sometimes it seems this Party ideal that men and women are equal only extends far enough to benefit the men! Women now must go to work along with men, as well as raise the children and keep the home. Men can fight each other in a fair way, but most women don't have a chance of overpowering a full-grown man. In this case, it's more of a predator/prey relationship than anything approaching equality, especially because most of the girls in my platoon are innocent! It fills me with a sort of blackness, but what can we do?

9.4.44, 21:30

We went into a different trench today, watching an open field where the German scouts have been seen sneaking across to spy on us, or ambush a gun or tank. It was a long day of watching.

Lida was my partner again, with Sasha and Kali just down the line, which made for good company. They've been paired up for two months now, and it seems to be working well, with Sasha as sniper far more often than Kali, who is usually spotter. To be sure, Kali has a great eye, but she's also a solid sharpshooter, just as good as Sasha, and I wonder why they don't switch it up more often. In truth, the more senior sniper often acts as spotter, because they know what to look for, but Sasha and Kali are the same level. Everyone in our platoon has the around same amount of experience, so we take turns. Maybe Sasha's eyes are not as good. Eye strain can be a serious problem for snipers. Only think how hard for the eyes, to scan the horizon constantly for every tiny movement.

Not long after we got settled into position, as the sun was rising, Sasha needed to use the latrine.

"We just got here!" I complained. Sasha knew it was dangerous to leave the trench in daylight. And not just for her! She'd put everyone in danger.

"I'm dying," she pleaded.

I wanted her to use the trench latrine, but she just groaned and said she had her monthly and needed rags. I knew she was being honest—the army doesn't provide anything to help us manage—but getting the platoon killed seemed the bigger danger. Sasha thought I was being dramatic, and *really* wanted to go, with the promise to be extra careful and slink like a snake through the mud. I almost laughed at that, Yulia. Impossible to imagine Sasha deliberately wallowing in the mud, given how tidy she is with her uniform, but she was determined.

"Keep your butt down," I said. Sasha laughed, hugged me and crept out the back of the trench.

It was strange when Sasha hugged me, because nobody else gives out hugs and I'm not used to it. Even you, Yulia, who are filled up with love from head to toe, you don't go around hugging people.

Perhaps it shows a friendly spirit—certainly Sasha is friendly, but I don't think I like it. Am I supposed to hug back? What are the rules? Some girls even kiss on the mouth, and for a long time, not just a peck, but they don't hug. Only Sasha.

With Sasha gone and the action slow, Lida and I took turns attaching sticks and leaves to the top of our helmets with mud, one keeping watch while the other built up the disguise. This we also learned in sniper school, how to make our helmets blend into the landscape when we stick our heads above the trench line. Lida laughed when I put my helmet on, calling me Bushhead, but I saw she wasn't being unkind, and I laughed too.

Lida is small, and I've wondered more than once how she was sorted out as a Queen. The army sorts us out as Queens or Pencils, you know, according to size. Everyone in our platoon is a Queen, except Lida, who is neither tall nor stout, but she's strong and wiry in her smallness, and I'm glad to have her because she's a very good spotter. Also a hard worker, constantly scanning. She kept up the search today, even with no sign of action, and even spotted something.

"In the tree at eleven o'clock," she said. "Maybe a sniper?"

A sniper! Excitement pulsed through me—a Fritz sniper! What a prize that would be. But then I remembered Sasha, somewhere outside the trench, possibly making her way back. What if she was spotted? I grabbed my binoculars and scanned the horizon out the rear of the trench. No Sasha. I turned to Lida and reminded her about Sasha, and we both got very serious about stalking our prey, hoping to get the business done before she got back.

We tilted our binoculars over the side of the trench and scanned the area at eleven o'clock.

"He moved again," Lida exclaimed, and I saw it too, something had moved in that tree!

I switched over to *Zhanna* (I've settled on *Zhanna d'ark*[11] for my Mosin, hoping I can channel her fierceness) and angled her slowly, carefully toward the tree, with millimeter movements so that the sunlight would not flash on the metal and create a target. I squinted, eyes frozen half-open, straining into the scope, scanning the branches where we'd seen something move. A flash of sunlight on the right side of my scope caught my attention, some kind of disturbance in the leaves, and I adjusted with hyper caution, as if the target was ten meters away rather than 300, and peering carefully through the scope, I saw a black squirrel, flicking his bushy tail.

A squirrel! I slumped down from my post and rested against the back of the trench. I looked at Lida, whose eyes were still glued to her 4x binoculars. She lowered them and gave me an apologetic look. I laughed hard, but tried to be quiet. "I hope Sasha will be safe from that squirrel," I snorted. "They have sharp little teeth!"

"Hey Bushhead, at least I spotted something," she said, but then she laughed too, and we both collapsed with silent giggles.

It's impressive that she spotted a squirrel from 300 meters, if you think about it. They're small creatures!

Sasha was lucky that there was no action while she was gone, only a few minutes of worry, and I know now that I shouldn't have let her leave. She's my friend, and I didn't want to disappoint her, but if another girl had asked this favor, would my answer have been the same? Not likely. I can see it's tricky, being boss to a friend. Going forward, I'll remember the squirrel who could have been a sniper, and not let anyone leave their position.

---

11   *Zhanna d'ark,* or Joan of Ark, was propagandized as a "warrior martyr" by the Communist Party, and became a cherished role model for the Soviet girl snipers.

10.4.44, 22:43

We went back into the same trenches today, watching the same field, but it was not boring. Cannon and artillery fire whistled above our heads from about five minutes after our feet hit the muck at the bottom. This was the first time I've experienced combat gunfire so close, ear shattering and persistent, launched from very near our trenches, which are the first line of defense near the German camp. It was a serious situation, Yulia, but somehow, I wasn't afraid. If anything, it was thrilling, I felt alive. *Fear has big eyes*, they say, but we fear different things. I was scared to death when I had to make my way through the *taiga*[12] on that cold night in 1938, after Papa kicked me out. Or when Fyodor was sent off to war and I was alone in Arkhangelsk. What is the sound of shells whistling past in comparison? It can't touch me.

The girls who've been fighting for a long time were fine today, the gunfire just gravel under their feet, but the newer girls, the ones who came to war around the same time that I did, they were afraid. Masha Komarova was a mess.

"Are they shooting at us?" she cried, when the first shells streaked over our heads. I looked down the line, but no Masha. I couldn't see her because she was crouching in the mud with her hands over her ears, far beneath the trench line.

"*Nyet*, they're after the guns," Kali said calmly. "But stay down, don't give them a target."

No one wanted one of those big shells to hit our trench, so we grew quiet as death, waiting and watching to see what would happen. Our own big guns were set up about 200 meters behind us, and the German guns were closer, maybe 100 meters in front of us. Like Kali said, they were after our guns, and didn't know we

---

12   *Taiga:* the coniferous forests of Northern Russia.

were there, but if they found us, they'd be very pleased to blow us to pieces. The Germans hate snipers. Their orders are to "take no sniper prisoners," to kill us instantly.

By mid-afternoon, the Germans had not tried to cross the field, but were still sending endless shells over our heads toward our guns. The day settled into a pattern, with Lida or I sticking our head above the trench line, scoping out targets, while the other hovered low in the mud, ears covered against the whine of enemy mortar shells passing over our heads. We switched back and forth, back and forth, when suddenly we heard the screech of our own shells going in the opposite direction, toward the enemy camp. Our guys were firing back at the Germans, and there was my platoon, stuck in the crossfire, not far from the target!

"Let's get out of here, they're going to kill us!" Masha shrieked, and started up the side of the trench, looking ready to make a run for it.

"*Stoy!*[13] Keep quiet and stay put if you want to live," I hissed fiercely, and then, more calmly, "no one is aiming at us."

Masha was right, we were in hot soup, but how would flying off in a panic help? What if the Germans spotted her leaving? We'd all be dead.

No, we needed to keep our heads. Suddenly Kali was next to me, with Sasha at her elbow.

"Our guys don't know we're here," Kali said. "Do you have a field telephone?"

I looked about wildly but knew that I didn't have one. Snipers don't carry telephones! Even I, as commander, carry the least that I possibly can, so that I can move quickly.

---

13   *Stoy:* Russian for stay, or stop.

Kali wanted to know how we could tell the boys they were shooting at us, and I could only wonder how they didn't know! We had orders to be there, how could they not know?

Sasha said that her boyfriend, Toska, knew where we were, because she had told him this morning, but he hadn't told her where he'd be, so we didn't know if he was on the gun line behind us. So frustrating! Because if he was with the gunners shooting up the field, he would see our danger and sound the alert. Why hadn't she thought to ask?

We heard the distant whistle of another volley of mortar shells headed in our direction, and I listened as their whisper became a shriek, hoping that I could somehow tell where they would land by their sound alone. The earth shuddered beneath our feet with the impact of the mortar. It seemed so close, like maybe twenty meters away, but it was hard to be sure, tucked down into the trench.

I itched all over with anxiety as I watched the girls crawl through the narrow ditches toward our end of the trench line. They looked terrified, and when I caught anyone's eye, I saw they were looking to me for answers.

I tore through our options. We could wait it out and hope we didn't get hit by a shell, make a run for it and hope the Nazis didn't gun us down, or I could escape, hope to not be seen, run to the line of guns and get a ceasefire. As commander, there was a better chance the gunners would listen to me. If I could get there.

"I'll go," I said. It was the obvious choice. I saw Kali nod at my words. She agreed with my decision.

I grabbed my gun, slung it over my shoulder, gulped down some water from my canteen, and scurried out the back.

The artillery guns were about 200 meters directly east of our trench line, with open field between us and them, and forests on either side. I wasn't brave or stupid enough to run directly across the meadow, so I belly crawled to the trees on the north side, which seemed my closest source of cover, and once there, I ran flat out through the trees until I reached the line. I was stopped there for a moment, awed by the sight of gun after gun as far as I could see, giant metal beasts on chain wheels that spat fire out one end and rockets out the other. Each gun was manned by a team of four or five guys, who all seemed to be very busy with running ammo from the cargo trucks, loading it into the cannons, and firing them. When a gunner close to me started cranking the firing switch, I came to my senses and yelled at him to stop. What if this was the shell that would go slightly astray and destroy my platoon? The gunner shot me a look, almost annoyed, and continued cranking the switch.

I ran back and forth behind the line, searching for an officer or anyone with the power to order the gunners to stand down. And suddenly—

"Little girl, what are you doing here?"

A shiver ran down my spine. *Little girl? Are you kidding me?* I turned around to look at this *mudak*, and what do you think? It was Blokhin. The big man himself. I knew him instantly, having seen his photo at headquarters, but this was the first time I'd seen him in the flesh. He was big as a bear, with a booming loud voice and bushy black eyebrows. Now he was coming toward me with a heavy step.

For a second, I was discombobulated, and put my hand out, instinctively, to stop him barreling into me. What was I doing here? What did I need to say?

And then I remembered. In a rush of words, I let him know my platoon was in the line of fire and begged him to order the gunners to stand down until nightfall, when my snipers could sneak out in the dark.

He stared at me with big knitted eyebrows, and then seemed to understand, his mouth an "O" of surprise, and he began to bellow at his troops. *"Ceasefire! Ceasefire!* Kasantsev, where are you, you motherfucker?"

A muddy-haired boy ran up, long and skinny. Blokhin barked out the ceasefire order again, and Kasantsev hurried off to send the command across the line.

I heaved a sigh and felt my shoulders relax. I had delivered the message. They would stop firing toward the trench, stop sending missiles of death in the general direction of my friends. But I couldn't be really comfortable until the Germans fired again, until I knew for sure that they hadn't seen me escape, that they wouldn't target the trenches.

"Who are you, little girl?" Blokhin asked.

God and Hell! *Little girl* again. I swallowed my annoyance and answered the question. He asked if I had pulled myself out of the trench to save the others, and nodded grimly when I said I had. "Welcome to the fight, Sergeant Shanina."

The fiddlers[14] went quiet after the ceasefire order, and we heard the Germans fire back at us almost instantly. Opportunists, they are.

"Incoming!" came the cry from a voice about fifty meters to the south, and I saw Blokhin hurl himself behind a long abatis that'd been built behind the line. I knew I should do the same, but I hesitated, wanting to see where the bombs were headed. If they hit the trench, my heart would die along with my friends. I crouched to the ground and scanned the skies anxiously, looking for plumes of smoke or shells or anything that stood out, and just barely spotted something gray hurtling through the air when it crashed into the ground about fifteen meters in front of me with tremendous force, like a mountain dropped from the sky, cratering into the earth, splintering shrapnel out sideways in a giant arc, so close that I could hear the jagged pieces of metal slicing the air. It was over before I knew it started, and I dove behind the abatis and took some deep

---

14   "Fiddlers" is a slang term for the gunners in the Red Army.

breaths. I was lucky to have all my limbs, but at least I knew they weren't targeting the trenches.

When the shells paused, I slunk back through the woods to a spot close to my platoon, lied down, and waited. It took a couple of hours for the sun to set far enough to cast its shadow over the trench, and then the girls showed up in the woods, one by one, anxious, grateful, and more than a little riled up by having been put in such danger. But they didn't seem to blame me, which is great. In fact, they seemed more appreciative of me. I think I gained some respect with them, and maybe even with Blokhin, who I'd gotten to meet face-to-face. I'm not sure about him yet. You know how much I hate foul language, and I hated him calling me "little girl" when I'm as tall as a lot of the boys out here. He didn't make me nearly as angry as that captain in Moscow, but still, it's not that different, is it? Lack of respect for females. We are soldiers, Yulia, and just like every boy out here, we live and die for the Motherland.

I'm glad that our scare came to nothing, but what a horrible feeling, to know that we could be killed by friendly fire! Because where's the glory in that?

16.4.44, 21:37

New orders today. We're to move to Kozie Gory for a special assignment, a counter-offensive, leaving day after tomorrow. *Hurrah!* It sounds like a really interesting job, and I've heard of this place, Kozie Gory. I think Sergei was there, when he first went into the NKVD. You would remember, Yulia.

Ah, Sergei! Hard to think of him in prison, but still—there's nothing I can do. Not yet.

My sniper tally is now five dead Hitlerites, and I'm getting better at it. Not the shooting part, which is the same as ever, but the brooding part. I've learned to shut off my thoughts, and as long as I stay busy, I can sleep at night. Another reason I'm eager to go on this mission — to keep moving.

Excited for our "special assignment." Sounds important, no?

19.4.44
An upper bedroom of the great house at Kozie Gory
(Lost my stupid watch)

Finally at Kozie Gory, after two days of marching. The first day was fine, with plenty of sunshine and one short rain shower, ending with the good feeling that comes over a body after a long march. But today… By God, Yulia, the devil was upon us. It rained hard all night, so we started off on tired feet, but it wasn't a bad morning. The afternoon was a year long. I spent the whole time wishing for the ZIS[15] we'd been promised, which would have shortened our hell, but someone decided we would walk, as there were "too many soldiers to transport a short distance." We marched with a slew of other infantry, like yesterday, in a long skinny line, no head nor tail in sight, Lida in front of me and Sasha behind, slinking our way through the forests on the northern side of the highway, when a foul stink assaulted our noses. So awful! I have no words. Decaying flesh, which is nothing new, since we have our own Dead Man's Woods near camp, but this time, many more bodies! Russian boys

---

15 ZIS were 4x2 Soviet transport trucks made in Moscow from 1932–1948 and used mostly for troop transport.

and girls who laid down their heads to win Smolensk when it was too cold to bury them, now caught in the spring thaw.

Sasha thought they were casualties from the battle that took place here last October–November. Five months ago. How many days is that, 150? 150 days of being buried in snow, beaten by rain, cooked in the sun, and half lost to the mud. I thought of our brothers, Fedya and Mikhail, whose bodies were never recovered, and found myself searching for a resemblance on the bloated faces, but it was hard to look and smell and not vomit, so I stopped. I wrapped my scarf over my nose and mouth, like before, but the stench was still disgusting. We hustled along, no talking, no noise, only the sound of mud trying to suck the boots off our feet. I focused on my boots and kept them swinging forward, but my nose was full of death, and somehow it got into my mouth and I had to swallow it.

"Oh God," Lida moaned, about three hours in. "How much longer?"

"Can't be much further." We'd been walking all day, how much further could it be?

Just after I had this thought, it began to rain. The line groaned, halted. We dug out our *plash palatkas*,[16] tossed them over our heads and rucksacks, and slogged on, one foot in front of the other. Not long after the rain started, the stink eased up, like a gift, like Baba Yaga[17] had taken pity and washed the filth away. I sucked air deep into my lungs and willed it to replace the foulness. The corpses began to thin out, and disappeared entirely an hour later, when we saw camp on the horizon, a snug little nest in the hills. Everyone cheered, feeling that we had clawed our way from hell back to a world for the living.

---

16 *Plash palatkas:* tarps/ponchos issued to all Red Army troops.
17 Baba Yaga is an old witch of the forest who plays a prominent role in Slavic folklore. She can destroy and kill, or she may play savior.

I almost melted with relief to learn that we'd be stationed in the Great House, which they call a *dacha*[18] but it's much grander than any *dacha* I've seen. It's a proper country manor, belonging to the NKVD, with fourteen rooms and a magnificent *banya* with steam and plenty of hot water.

We went to the bath before dinner, and it was *glorious*! "Almost makes up for that march," Sasha said, sighing into the hot water, and she was right. It's so hard to be clean out here, Yulia. You take those things for granted, normally, but to be honest, I haven't been outside these clothes in a week, and this was the first real bath I've had since I got to the Front. I wished I had clean clothes to put on after, but we can't have everything.

All the girls were so much more cheerful after our visit to the *banya*.[19] A fresh start, that's what we needed, and how wonderful that we'll have access to the bath the whole time we're here.

We had dinner at the Great House, which felt a little like eating out in a fancy restaurant, although the food was the same stew with potatoes as always. The house used to be a holiday resort for the Tsar, and for other rich people from Smolensk, and after Red October, it was used by party officials until the Germans invaded and took it over. Now it's ours again, after the victory at Smolensk. So much fighting over this little spot on the earth, but the house is perfect, undamaged! Some of the artillery guys were saying that it's protected by magic but I think they were playing with us, or stupid, or something. Most likely it's never been targeted. Who would want to see this fine house destroyed when it makes such a great headquarters? Whatever the truth is, I feel safe here, and I like imagining Lenin rambling around the grounds, or watching

---

18   *Dacha:* a Russian country house or cottage that's used as a second home.
19   *Banya:* a Russian sauna, often used as a steam house.

a film in the cinema. Maybe he slept in the same bedroom where my platoon is situated. *Chjort!*[20]

The land outside is not in good shape. We're in the middle of a forest, with a river running through it, but half the trees have been blown up, turned into burnt sticks, others with helmets wedged deep in their trunks. Papa would hate to see the death of this forest. *We are guests of the land*, I can hear him say. War is not concerned with being a good guest, Papa. But the river Dnieper is beautiful still, with the kind of peaceful energy that comes from being always on the move.

Colonel Degtyarev is in charge around here. He seems good for a brass type, not too full of himself, not rude, and he gave out orders straight and clear. My platoon will keep watch from the upper windows of the house to support a blocking action, which is perfect for us, since the top floor has a good view in all directions. The primary directive—"defend the house."

We are to keep watch around the clock, and tonight that will be tough, after marching two days solid with a few minutes of sleep in between. Last night, the rains drove into our *plash palatkas* while we curled beneath, in a puddle, bone-tired from our march. I didn't sleep well. Lida and Masha volunteered for first watch tonight, so I'm stretched out on my bedroll which I've laid out on top of a thick carpet, hoping for some rest before I take second shift. It's very comfortable, and I'm very tired. I've had to force myself awake long enough to write out our day, but for you, Yulia, I'm happy to do it. And I'm happy that it's done.

---

20   *Chjort:* a mild Russian expletive, similar to "dang."

21.4.44
Kozie Gory

I felt like I'd just closed my eyes when I was jolted awake by the sound of gunfire, very loud, very near. I jumped up and grabbed my rifle.

"So close!" Sasha cried, and she was right. The shots seemed to come from within the house itself. Had the Nazis gotten inside? And what happened to Lida and Masha, on first watch?

I peered carefully over the sill into the pitch-black night. It took a minute for my eyes to adjust, and then I saw them, maybe thirty Fritzes, crawling up the southern hill toward the front of the house, three of them almost directly beneath my window. Lida appeared at my side, scoping out the scene, with her hair mussed and her eyes rough with sleep.

"God and Hell, Lida!" I exclaimed, but she gave me such a torn up, guilty look that I stopped there.

Suddenly there was a great distant boom, followed by the fast-growing metallic whistle of a cannon, and an explosion to the northwest, where the artillery guys were set up. In a flash, these good guys became part of a burning hole in the ground! My heart felt like a school bell clanging in my chest—we were under attack! Half the girls panicked, grabbed their things and dashed for the door.

"Get to your posts! Shoot them down!" I yelled. They couldn't just leave! What were they thinking?

I readied *Zhanna* and positioned her barrel on the window ledge, with sights on the closest Fritz. Without thought or hesitation, I shot him in the head, *For Fedya*, and moved on to the next. *For Mikhail.*

"Get them while they're crawling," I cried, and sent my third bullet into its mark.

Kali was second to react, shooting from the southern window. The other girls soon followed, Sasha and Lida covering the western windows, the others racing off to their posts in the north and east rooms. We picked them off, one after another, and before long the few that remained scurried back to their den, somewhere deep in the forest. I kept the buttocks of one Fritz in my sights as he ran, and imagined giving him a real pain in the rear. But I didn't shoot, which is interesting. I thought I would.

I got eleven kills that night, the night before last, acting on instinct alone, without thought or plan. And it felt good, not dirty. I guess it's cleaner to shoot to kill when your friends' lives are in danger.

Next morning, no one had any idea that we slept through first watch, but everyone knew we defended the house successfully. I was glad to skip a reprimand, and in fact Colonel Degtyarev praised us for quick actions, singling me out for killing eleven fascists in one skirmish, which meets the criteria for the Order of Glory. The *Order of Glory*, Yulia! Can it be possible? I want to believe.

Later, I had a talk with Lida and Masha about falling asleep on the job. I wasn't too mean, but I made sure they realized that we'd almost certainly have been killed in our beds if the cannons hadn't woken us. So careless! But I think it won't happen again. We lost five men and one 152 mm Howitzer in the explosion that roused us, and several more dead and wounded, but they lost many more, and such is war. I'm glad that we were part of the counter-attack, and for myself, how do I feel? I don't have any trouble shooting fascists now—thank the gods that feeling has passed. I feel… useful, perhaps for the first time in my life. I guess I'm good at this.

26.4.44
Kozie Gory

My little grey book has nineteen kills recorded. I wonder how long I can keep this up? Just last night, I thought I was fine with it, with killing people like it's nothing. I want that feeling back, because what good can come from brooding over life and death, and why I've been turned into a god with the power to decide who gets which? Power. The root of evil is power, Yulia, not money, although plenty get the two confused.

I'm getting more accustomed to death being everywhere. Those bodies in the woods, the artillery guys by the shed, the Germans we shot down as they crawled up the hill. There are a bunch of mass graves full of dead Poles around here, with NKVD milling around, and that's a different kind of death because we don't know how or why those Poles were killed, only that it happened a couple years ago. Until this morning, our platoon has been too busy killing and defending to have time to think about the graves, but now that Fritz has retreated further, our job has hit a lull.

We were happy to have a proper breakfast today, after the sun had risen. A good, hot *kasha*,[21] which Sasha, Kali and I took at a table in the kitchen that was shoved up against a big window. My eyes kept returning to two big dirt mounds that were framed by the window, at the edge of the forest. Three NKVD agents were stationed there, guarding the area, and their efforts to keep people away seemed to be successful, as there was some new growth scattered on the mounds. But why would old graves show fresh growth, and why were they being guarded?

"What's the story behind those graves," I wondered out loud, and Kali had a lot to say on the subject. It seems that the woods

---

21 *Kasha:* a breakfast porridge typically made with buckwheat or wheat, berries and honey.

surrounding the Great House are known as Katyn Forest, a name that has become famous in the papers as a place of execution, the place where the Nazis executed thousands of Polish people and dumped them into mass graves. Later, Germany tried to blame it on us, claiming that they found the mass graves accidentally after they took possession of the land in 1942, that they dug them up and found all the bodies, and reburied them. Our government denied everything and did some research to prove that it was the Germans who did the killing.

I listened to Kali with a feeling of dread, thinking of Sergei's letter. What had he said? He'd done hard and terrible things. Sergei had been stationed here, at Kozie Gory, I was pretty sure of it. Did some of those "terrible things" have to do with the executions that took place here?

Kali was continuing on, talking about the investigation report, which she'd read from cover to cover. Local farmers made statements about German trucks carrying loads of prisoners into Katyn in 1942, during Nazi occupation. Beekeepers heard gunshots. Scientists found "forensic evidence," whatever that means, and they found letters and papers on the bodies that were dated from the time of German occupation.

I got more and more agitated as Kali spoke. What had Sergei been forced to do, and *why*? What reason could they have for coercing statements out of locals unless it was actually our side that put those people in the graves? Never before have I been tempted to share the contents of Sergei's letter with Sasha and Kali, but at that moment, I had to fight against the urge, because I wanted their opinion, I wanted to get to the truth of it.

But I didn't want to believe that Russians had killed those Poles. Why would we?

Sasha asked why the Nazis would want to make it seem like we had executed all those people, and then immediately answered her own question with "Who can guess why they do anything? They're so strange! They don't think like us."

This is true, Yulia, and I wouldn't put anything past them. Maybe they'd threatened the locals, with death or dismemberment or whatever else, and the NKVD had to persuade them to get over the threats.

I remember my first *Komsomol*[22] meeting in Arkhangelsk, where posters of the Nazi beasts were taped to the walls, half-human, half-savage, blood dripping from yellow fangs. How can we know what they're thinking or planning? We know only that they hate us, and they like killing, so why not kill those Poles and blame it on us? I said as much to Sasha, and she nodded grimly, but Kali got tense, huffed out an angry breath and started rapping her fingers on the table.

"What did I say?" I wanted to know, but she just shook her head and looked down. Clearly, Kali knew something, and Sasha demanded aggressively that she tell us.

"I have to share every thought in my head?" Kali snapped back, and I groaned my complaint. If they were going to bicker, I was going to leave.

But then she heaved a great sigh, as if to say *Oh all right, I'll tell you*, and leaned in, and Sasha and I followed like horses to water. She looked back and forth between us, and said in a very low voice—"Truth is hard to find."

She said it expectantly, like it was an all-important proclamation, like we should fall to the ground in spasms of revelation or something, but I was a little disappointed. She seemed to sense this and went on to point out that the place was crawling with NKVD, which implied that the graves were important to the Party, that

---

22 The *Komsomol*, or All-Union Leninist Young Communist League, was the last of three communist organizations for Soviet youth. Kids graduated from the Little Octobrists at nine, the Young Pioneers at 14, and the Komsomol at 28.

there was something to hide. And how could we trust the results of the investigation, since it was conducted by the Soviet Union, whose interest was in proving its innocence?

"You think we killed those Poles, don't you?" Sasha whispered bluntly, laying bare what hung in the air.

And she does, Yulia. She admitted it. Kali thinks the NKVD killed and buried all those people, and covered it up. God knows why they would do such a thing, but that's what Kali thinks, and perhaps she's right. Perhaps Sergei helped them cover it up.

I asked how she could be sure, and she said she couldn't, that it was just what she thought and she didn't want to try to convince us it was true, because it was "safer to believe Stalin."

I looked at her, wanting to laugh but seeing no sign of humor on her face. As if we can choose what to believe! What about what really happened?

"Whatever you think happened, that's what happened."

I looked at Kali, amazed at what I was hearing. There IS a truth to be found! Those Polish people didn't shoot themselves and jump into holes in the ground. Someone killed them, and someone else didn't.

I wanted to say as much, wanted to tell Kali she was wrong, but then Sasha said loudly "Just take care to believe something that's good for you, right?"

Kali slashed her hand across her throat, motioning for silence, and seemed ready to be done with the conversation. The two remaining girls from our platoon got up to leave, and I waited until they were gone before I turned to Kali and asked how she, Kaleriya Petrova, had the power make something true by thinking it.

Kali rolled her eyes. That's not what she meant, she believes in the *istina*,[23] but what really matters is what we think is true.

---

23   *Istina:* Russian for objective, cosmic truth, differing from *pravda*, which refers to truth as we experience it through our senses and impressions.

"What really matters is the truth!" I said. How could Kali, so educated and intelligent, think differently? She looked like she'd just eaten a raw onion, but she wouldn't back down. She believed absolutely in what she was saying, that everybody gets different facts, and believes different things. That real truth is hard to find. Maybe impossible.

"You *believe* our secret police killed those Poles," I said.

"Yes, and I could be wrong, I could have bad facts. I can't know anything for sure."

I get what she was saying, Yulia. There are a lot of lies and false stories out there, but how does that take away from the real story? I've been lied to many times, and that makes the truth more important to me, not less.

"If a man's being chased by a pack of wolves, and jumps off a cliff to escape them, what does he care whether or not the wolves were real? He's dead," Kali said, still trying to get her point across.

I could only insist that the wolves were either there or they weren't, and that was important because if there were no wolves, that guy didn't need to die! But Kali said what difference does that make to the man who is dead?

I shook my head. Wasn't it self-centered to think your own thoughts were more powerful than the objective truth? "Shouldn't we discover the real truth, for the greater good?"

Kali laughed. "For the collective, lies are more useful than the truth," she said, and then she looked cross and sat up straighter, like she'd said something she didn't mean to say.

I leaned back, a little shocked to have it laid out so plainly, and worried my fingers over the wooden armrests of my chair, smooth as silk from generations of wear. Kali watched me steadily, her eyes bristling with concern for what I might be thinking. *Stalin killed those Poles, and Sergei was involved in the coverup* came bursting into my mind, sharply, like some part of me insisted I consider the idea although I wanted to push it away.

Sasha began to complain about our seriousness, saying that if Kali was right then she must also be wrong, and if none of us can know anything, why not stop talking about it and go to the *banya* while we still could? We all laughed, and that was the end of the conversation. I'm struck by it, and it feels heavy. I have no wish to hold onto it.

Do you remember Aleksander Yeltinov from the village? Such a good uncle, kind to me as a child, and I played with Masha at school. Then he was called *kulak*[24] and accused of stealing and hoarding, but our whole childhood, they never had any food! Next thing we heard, Yeltinov confessed, and Masha and the whole family disappeared. *Gone to Siberia*, came the whispers, and I began to wonder if he was a *kulak* after all, an Enemy of the People. But how could that be, when they were all skin and bones?

It separates us, those who respect the underlying truth, and those who accept the story they're fed. We can't talk openly, so it's not easy to know what's real, but it's there somewhere. It must be there, Yulia, there has to be a real truth that we can rely upon. I want to see clearly, to wipe away all of the lies and see the plain, naked truth, even if it's hard. But how do I do that?

---

24   *Kulak:* Russian for a peasant farmer who owned at least eight acres of land and employed workers, until Stalin announced the "liquidation of kulaks as a class" in December, 1929, after which the label *kulak* became an accusation for anyone the Party wanted to get rid of.

Yedma, Arkhangelsk Oblast

To Sgt. Roza Shanina
Western Front, Fifth Army, 184th Rifle
Division

My dear Roza,

I was so pleased to get your letter, folded into a lovely triangle, which Pavel tells me is a sign that the writer still lives. I'll be on high alert for triangles in the mail, as well as everywhere, now that they've become a beacon of hope. I'm sure I'll never look at them the way I used to.

I do wish your letter was a bit longer, but I suspect paper is difficult to come by. I don't complain, I know you're busy exterminating the enemy, but if you have the time and the paper, I would love to hear all the details about your new friends, Sasha and Kali, and how you are adapting to life at war. Papa will get me paper if I ask; I enclose a blank sheet here, and will send more when I can.

We're all anxious for the day when the enemy is driven out of Russia, and must practice patience until that time. Patience has become my lot in every way, and I find I'm mostly equal to it. I'm to stay here on the kolkhoz, rather than go on to technical school, at least until tuition becomes free again. Mama needs my help so very much, I don't see how I could leave anyway, with her hands and feet so very bad this spring. The poor thing is unable to do anything without suffering, so I've taken over almost all of her chores at the dairy and at home. She leans heavily on a new cane that Papa acquired for her, yet even with that, she can only hobble around, wanting to be useful and holding her breath against the pain. I look forward to the end of the rains, so that she can take herself in hand again. Anya is a great help to me, especially in the dairy, with quick feet and quicker smiles. I won't say "little Anya" any longer, because she is now nine years old, sturdy and well grown, a far cry from the waif who hid in her bed for two weeks without speaking to a creature.

Mama and I have been praying together when Papa is out of the house, mostly for you and Sergei, that you will stay safe and healthy, that your hardship might be borne lightly. When Pavel is deployed, we will add him to the list. Mama has been teaching me her old catechism, and it's a sweet time, her eyes brighten in a way I haven't seen elsewise. She's eager for me to learn, so that "God may one day come back into the family."

I've gone through the news first before answering your question, in the hope that watchful eyes will look past this letter. Pavel's friend's sister is a mail watcher, and she has told him that they don't look closely at letters from civilians, only those from soldiers, and that they often look at the beginning and the end and skip the middle entirely. I'm counting on that in writing the following!

Firstly, your memory is correct, our brother Sergei was at Kozie Gory with the NKVD, almost exactly one year ago. I remember this clearly because it was just after my sixteenth birthday, when he came for a visit from that place directly, and brought with him an old, pretty-bound reader of Pushkin's poems that he found there at the Great House, and gifted it to me.

Why me? I asked, because it seemed such a fine gift. You will take care of it, he said. Dear Sergei! He's right, I treasure it, and will be certain that no harm comes to it. "I do not quarrel with these dear chains, they don't demean," (from Rose Maiden, you know.)

But Sergei was changed on that visit. I felt that he'd gone through a rough time, but when I asked, he switched the topic. Naturally, I wouldn't want him to disclose anything that he shouldn't, but I confess that in my worry I pressed him slightly, and he did eventually share his story with me. Such a story, Roza! But I feel I must be brief. Our brother was there in the spring of 1943 as part of the investigation that was conducted to disprove the Germans' claim that the bodies found in mass graves at Katyn Forest had been killed in 1941, when the area was still under Soviet control. Dear Sergei, he didn't want to tell me anything about his experience, didn't want me to know anything that could bring me trouble, and it was only when I pointed out that I was quite safe under Papa's protection that he chose to confide in me.

Sergei started with You deserve a better brother, and went on to tell me such horrifying things, acts he was obliged to commit in his role as NKVD officer, mostly in the office of obtaining signed statements from farm folk who lived in the area. He persuaded them to testify that they saw Nazis bring in truckloads of prisoners to Kozie Gory, and heard gunshots go off at all hours for several weeks during the spring of 1942, when the Germans occupied the area. You will infer the ultimate meaning as to who is to blame for the thousands of executions that took place there.

I imagine that you, who have seen more of the world than I, have some idea of the methods of persuasion that were used.

I confess I've never heard anything so shocking in my whole life, and I can't bring myself to actually write down what Sergei told me. Indeed, I couldn't believe it at first, and felt sure there must be some dreadful misunderstanding. That such things could happen! That dear Sergei could be a perpetrator! But he was forced to it, and by keeping that in mind I've been able to prevent this information from shading my affection for our eldest brother. If you could have seen him Roza, he was so low! How very tragic for him, to be obliged to do things against his character! He left two days later, for Moscow, and I haven't seen him since. I will end here and write of other things.

Pavel leaves for Vsevobuch next month. We will all miss his accordion playing in the evenings, he's grown so talented! But he's excited to go, eager to join the fight against the fascist beasts. He's very young, Roza, barely sixteen. It's difficult for me to think of anyone younger than myself fighting as a soldier, much less our own dear little brother, but such is the time we live in. Once Pavel has gone it will be just myself, young Marat, and the orphans at home. I hold onto the hope that this war will end soon, and that you and Pavel will come back to Yedma, to this home. Naturally, Sergei will go back to Maria and Alexei in Moscow. But you are still young and unattached, Roza, and I'm certain that Papa would welcome you, as a war hero. He's not so very hard and strict as he used to be.

Simone, still Queen of the barn, has birthed a healthy calf, and we've named her Roza in your honor. Anya noticed yesterday that the cows were "cheerful to have a new baby," and I think she's right, clever girl! I never noticed this collective, mothering spirit before, but I see it now. Baby Roza is a sweet little cow, with big brown eyes. I'm as fond of her as any of her cow aunties can be.

I know how fierce you are, how much you want to fight for our comrades, and naturally you are fighting very hard to push the fascists out of the country. Please write to me when you return from your assignment and arrive safely back at camp. Exterminate the Enemy!

Tseluyu,[25]
Yulia

28.4.44
Vitebsk camp grounds, near billet

We got back from Kozie Gory very late last night so we have the day off. Such a beautiful day here — no rain! The sun warms my face, and I've had your letter this morning with the mail. Your news from home is just as it should be, except for the part about Sergei, which haunts me. I have a million questions for you, but we can't talk openly, and my scribbles in this journal are one-way rambles. I know that one day you'll read these words, and that keeps me going. I so wish that I could write a real letter to you about Sergei's arrest and imprisonment, but I can't. No good and much evil would come from it. Poor Sergei! He carries his life so heavily. I understand, I'm not so different — I fight against the heaviness every day.

It appears that Kali was right. I don't know how to think of the whole mess, about what it means for us soldiers. Exactly what are we fighting for? I also wonder why Sergei was so surprised by what

---

25 *Tseluyu*—a Russian sign-off for letters meaning "I am kissing you."

he was required to do as an NKVD agent. I understand why you would be shocked, Yulia, living in the quiet way that you do, surrounded by your books and your chores, but how could Sergei not know? Everyone understands the role of an NKVD agent–bully, enforcer, terrorist.

Kali may have been right about the graves at Katyn Forest, but she wasn't right to say that what we think is true is more important than what is really true. Sergei might have believed he was taking an easy job, but the truth came out in all its power, didn't it?

1.5.44

We're working with the communications guys for the next few days. This morning, we nearly froze crawling through a muddy swamp to reach their trenches, but managed to drop in before the sun had shown itself. Every time I crawl like this, on my belly, I think *Keep your butt down!* The instructors at sniper school would holler that all the time, it was their favorite thing, and then they'd whack us on the bottom with long sticks as we squirmed around like snakes. They weren't always horrible, Yulia, but that wasn't the most fun thing ever.

Today, we kept watch on a brigade of light tanks, the German Ferdinands, with orders to pick off any officers we could get a clean shot on. Identifying the officers is tricky, because they don't wear their rank. We have to read it in their postures, in the way they talk to other soldiers, or put their hands on their hips, and maybe point while giving an order. It was a long day, full of watching and waiting, but I did get one kill, and Sasha got one too. We have the same assignment tomorrow—will be interesting to see if the Nazis make any changes because we were picking them off today.

There's another matter that's on my mind, it seems silly, but it's sticking to my brain and I need to write about it. I met a boy over dinner, named Misha Panarin, but I acted the idiot. In my defense I haven't seen any boys my age for years, only uncles and children. Now I'm confused and embarrassed, because he's not uninteresting.

We got to the field kitchen on the early side of supper, Sasha, Kali and I, because there was no food runner for the trenches today and our stomachs gnawed at us. I took my *kulesh*[26] quickly, sitting cross-legged on the ground, as usual. Afterward, I leaned back on my elbows, enjoying my warm, full belly, when a tall, thin man of twenty-three or four walked up to us with his bucket.

"Hello, the snipers!" he said, nodding at everyone in our little cluster, then resting his eyes on me.

Sasha and Kali greeted him in a familiar way ("Misha!"), and invited him to sit with us. I guess they got to know him during the two months before I arrived, when some of the girls were working support for the artillery guys. Sasha has seen a lot of him, because he's a friend of her boyfriend Toska.

Misha crowded in between Sasha and myself, where there was just enough room to sit without touching either of us. They traded the regular greetings, and Misha told us he was feeling lucky to be alive because the gun team next to him had been blown up this morning.

Sasha tensed, because Toska is a gunner.

"Not Toska," Misha added, significantly. "Do you think I could sit here and smile if Toska'd been hit?" Turns out it was the unit of a new gunner, a Solzhenitzhen, but he was just wounded while his loaders had been blown to pieces, all three of them.

Misha grew serious, making a business out of fussing with his *kulesh* and sticking his nose down to smell it. "Could have been me, my gun. My guys."

---

26 *Kulesh*—Russian soup made with millet.

"But it wasn't," Sasha said.

Misha chuckled darkly. "Right. I borrowed some more time today. Odd, how the gods of war decide to crush one life over another." His eyes landed on me again, and he leaned in, very close. "A living and breathing *Zosia*," he murmured, under his breath, like he was thinking out loud.

Sasha and Kali exchanged a smirk, while I nudged away from him. He noticed this, seemed to realize that I was uncomfortable, because he moved back into his own space and took a few bites of soup. But I was curious, I had to ask — "What's a Zosia?"

"Goddess of war and beauty," he said, between bites.

I snorted, said "I'm not beautiful," and looked at him more closely. Who was this boy? He wasn't handsome in a traditional way, but he had fine, grey eyes and a polite manner, when he wasn't pushing in too close. Sasha argued that I was very pretty and maybe I just didn't know it, and Misha nodded.

Misha finished his soup and turned to me again, said that he knew who I was, that everyone did, because I'd been made commander fresh out of sniper school, and had earned a Medal of Glory just two weeks into my tour of duty. "Impressive and interesting," he said, with a look that made me believe that he meant it. Then he said that I must know that I'm beautiful. "How could you not know?"

"There are no young men left outside the war," Sasha answered for me, and Misha went "Ohhh" as if that hadn't occurred to him, then he said it was a crime for women to waste away, as "flowers that blush unseen," which made me think of you, Yulia, and your love of poetry.

But I wasn't so pleased with the message behind the comment, which implies that a woman is wasting away unless someone notices that she's beautiful. How rude! I think he was trying to be gallant or flirty or something, but it was a silly thing to say. The conversation in general made me unsettled, like I'd felt as a child lost in the *taiga*, scrabbling for landmarks, keeping an eye out for predators. I became very shy and didn't have any idea what to think or say, when finally something occurred to me — "I'd rather be known as a good shot."

"From the north!" Misha exclaimed, in a pleased way, and I wondered what he had to be pleased about. Was he happy to have recognized my accent, or happy that I'm a Northerner? Because who likes a northern dialect, except us *taiga* dwellers?

He went on to say that there could be no doubt that I was a great shot, and how lucky for me to be both beautiful and talented. This was too much for me. I mean, really? I rolled my eyes and said he was making an elephant out of a fly.

He didn't like being accused of sweet talk, and muttered something like "I'm not a flatterer" and got up to leave shortly after. "Don't be a stranger," Sasha called after him, and he waved and was gone.

I watched him go, and wondered what had happened.

Sasha turned to me with a look of exasperation, asking why I was so unfriendly toward him. But I didn't think I was unfriendly, more like cautious, because he made me nervous.

"Misha's a good guy," Sasha said, "and he sure seemed to like you."

God and Hell, I bungled the whole thing. But he made me nervous! Sasha and Kali seem to really like him, and I trust their opinion. There is something about him, something that isn't loathsome. But really, the Goddess of War and Beauty? How was I supposed to respond to that? Simper and bat my eyelashes, maybe giggle? That's not going to happen, Yulia. I'm not built that way.

I wonder if Misha Panarin is actually interesting, and if he isn't, who would be the right kind of man for me? Do you remember that dandelion game we made up, years ago? *Blow three times, he'll never have money. Blow two times, you'll marry someone funny. Blow just once, he'll treat you sweet as honey.*

How embarrassing. But we were children. I remember one afternoon in the field behind Aunt Agnes' pig sty, we must have blown a hundred dandelions, trying to get all the seeds off in one blow to improve our chances of getting a good husband. That seems a hundred years ago, when we were sure we'd each find a boy and get married, raise a family. It used to be that when I saw dandelions, I thought of boys, but now I think only of you, and our childish dreams. Maybe big dreams never die, because now I want to go ask a dandelion about Misha Panarin.

Here is the last page of this notebook. I don't know if I'll be able to find another. Technically, we're not allowed to keep diaries, although I'm not the only one who does. I'd ask you to send another notebook, but it would never reach me, and it might alert the army that I'm keeping an illegal journal. I hope this isn't the end of it! How will I manage my thoughts and feelings if I can't write them down?

SECOND JOURNAL:
SUMMER

15.5.44
Sniper billet, Vitebsk

I was able to get a notebook after all, and from Misha Panarin, of all people. Yes, we've been spending time together, and I find my thoughts and eyes are on him very often. I've also been thinking of you, Yulia, and wondering if you're happy in Yedma with Mama and Papa and Marat and the orphans. For me, happiness is a white hare in the snow. It leaves footprints, sometimes I catch a glimpse, but it seems impossible to catch. And what would I do with it if I had it? I'm not sure I know how to be happy.

I think of Yedma, with its endless forests and rivers. I miss the trees, and the honey, and the fresh milk. Oh! I'm craving some now. But I've been gone from there such a long time. Arkhangelsk has been my home for almost six years now, and when I was asked to write down a home address for the army, I put in the Kindergarten #2. Seems strange, to use my workplace as a home address, but the little apartment at the Kindergarten #2 is the last place I lived, before I left for Vsevobuch. It was a sad and bare box, and I don't miss it, but I do think of my students, and of Anna Tamarova. She was so kind to me, Yulia, really a good person. I hope she's well, that all my students are well.

La, so nostalgic! There's been a lot of rain lately, which always makes me serious. But I'm sure my mood comes from having no orders today or yesterday, nothing to do but sit around and stew. There's been a "shake up" of the Fifth Army, everyone relabeled and re-assigned, with my platoon stuck in the rear. I'm now Senior Sergeant, which is nice, but I'd trade it in a second for some action. I asked Blokhin to give me a job, any combat job at all, but he refused. It seems policy change includes a new rule that women aren't allowed on the frontlines of battle.

"Comrade Captain, how are we supposed to spend our time?" I asked.

Blokhin shrugged. "Curl your hair," he suggested.

I imagined myself scratching his eyes out. Yes, I'm a bit on edge. Discouraged, and desperately bored. My skin crawls with the need to move, to shoot, to continue on the path I started down on April 2nd.

Then I asked if I could get leave, since I wasn't needed in combat. I could finally get rid of Sergei's letter! But he shot that down as well. Why? I haven't been active long enough to request leave. I can't work and I can't leave, and Sergei will have to rot a little longer.

Sasha and Kali don't seem to mind the lull. I love them, but I don't understand their thinking. Kali was actually cheerful today as she went around making "improvements" to the billet, new curtains that she sewed up from gauze and dyed in quinine. She sweet-talked the medical unit into giving her the supplies. They are bright, bright yellow—almost hurts my eyes to look at them. I don't know, maybe it's an improvement. Everyone seems to think so. They make Kali happy, and that's worth something.

I'm the outsider in the platoon, the only one who hates the new rules. Apart from Misha, who is a little bright spot, I'm bereft of everything. Of my friends' understanding, of a sense of purpose, even of my own conviction. How can I be a great and extraordinary warrior if I'm not allowed to fight?

This afternoon, I was falling the deep way into a great sulk, when a reporter from the army newspaper *Destroy the Enemy* arrived at our billet. He was a tall guy, bony like a skeleton, named Pyotr Malchonov. Not a good-looking guy, Pyotr, with his great crooked nose and bad teeth, and eyes so intense that I felt he could see all my secrets, but I liked him anyway. He seemed interesting.

He asked to speak with me. So surprising! I invited him into the billet, sat down at the great table and waited for him to tell me what he was after. He folded his long body into a chair across from me, leaned forward onto his elbows and looked at me closely, his eyes traveling all over my face.

"Sergeant Shanina," he said, "you're standing out in the crowd. The first female soldier of the Fifth Army to win a Medal of Glory. I'd love to follow your career in *Destroy the Enemy*."

I was shocked. The first female! I'd be lying if I said I wasn't flattered. Such a feeling, to be treated like I was a person of importance! I've never known it before. I agreed to an interview, but didn't want my photograph in the newspaper, although he continued to push for it.

"I don't want to be the center of attention," I said.

He leaned back in his chair and pulled a cigarette case from his pocket. He pulled out two store-bought cigarettes with his lips, lit them with a shiny gold lighter, and handed one to me, saying "Call me Pyotr."

I took the cigarette, and noticed his smile, like a friendly banner waving from his face. Smiles are so pleasant, but they're not common, not the Russian way. More people should smile, like Pyotr, and Sasha. I'm going to try to smile more often.

Pyotr tilted back further on the legs of his chair, smoking and watching me with his intense blue eyes, and started talking about how fame and attention can be dangerous, but can also have its perks.

"Like what, execution?" I asked.

I had surprised him, and he laughed deeply, which caused him to go into a coughing fit. I asked him if he never worried that something he wrote would be used against him.

"I need to be careful not to do anything stupid," he said. "But beyond that, who is safe? I don't let fear make decisions."

Shrewd, I thought. And yet, things change so quickly, and what's popular today could land you in a work camp tomorrow. We talked about this, about being in the spotlight, about the whisperers, for quite a while. I found him very interesting, Yulia, and in the end, I told him he could put my picture in the paper with his article. Because really, who cares? The rules are different now that I'm at war. Every day, I wake up ready to die for the cause, if necessary.

He was pleased, and whistled as he walked to the door to call the photographer. When he returned, he slipped a letter from his pocket and slid it across the table toward me.

"I know your brother's jailor," he said, by way of explanation.

"What—" I began, but Malchonov shook his head slightly, and touched his forefinger to his lips. I pushed down a rush of anxiety over what the letter might contain and tucked it into my breast pocket.

The photographer set up outside and got shots of the entire platoon under the one great tree that still grows in our yard, and several of me posing this way and that, in full uniform with my rifle. When the photos had all been taken and the interview was over, the two newsmen packed up to leave. Malchonov promised to send a copy of the newspaper when my interview is published, and with a quick salute, he was gone.

Dear Roza,

How are you? Is the war still turning our way? I've been isolated for a long time now with no news except what my jailor passes on. It seems like years since I was at the frontlines, although it's only been a few months. At least my new jailor is nicer than the last one. He brought a letter from

Maria, written from well outside Moscow, to my relief. Did you get my letter to Papa? I live in terror that I will be tried before Papa has a chance to intervene. Perhaps he got the letter and chose to ignore it, but I don't want to believe that. Hope is my only defense against insanity.

I've learned the real reason I was arrested, and like I suspected, it's all Beria. Few know his true nature, his contempt for all human life excepting his own, his sick enjoyment of inflicting pain, of rape, of murder, but I have seen it with my own eyes.

I hesitate to write this down, to burden you with it, but my life is at stake, and now there is little Alexei to think of, as well as Maria. It concerns Beria, and my service to him for the six months I was assigned to Moscow. One of my duties was to deliver girls to him, and I'm sorry to say that I performed this duty for a time, despite knowing how bad the experience would be for the girls. Beria's office is soundproofed, and no one knows exactly what goes on inside, but the girls came out changed. Broken. Sometimes bleeding. Sometimes they came out a different door, dead, with purple bruises on their necks. The dead ones were buried in the back of the Lubyanka's rose garden, the others got a bouquet of flowers from that same garden before getting dropped back on the streets. One night, when I wasn't working, Maria and I were strolling through Gorky Park, shortly before we married, and came across Beria. He looked Maria up and down, scrutinized her really, and the next night he ordered casually that I bring Maria to his office. I said no, said that we were to be married, thinking that Beria would change his mind if he knew Maria was of personal importance to me, but he just stood in front of me, still as a statue, and then adjusted his glasses and turned away in silence. He then asked my partner Niko to fetch him Maria, and Niko being a very good friend, told me of the order. I left the Lubyanka immediately, went straight to Maria and put her on a train out of the city, toward her father's farm. And so, I'm a traitor, but I'm not sorry for my actions. There is nothing on this earth that would get me to hand Maria over to that monster.

It's true that I've become a foul creature. I feel the truth of that. I wonder at my ability to deliver those other girls, who must have been dear to someone. I sought to erase my own thoughts and think only for Mother Russia, but how could anyone with a brain not wonder how the torture, rape and murder of young girls strengthens Russia, or furthers the transition to true Communism?

Perhaps I deserve to die. Perhaps that would be better for my son, now six months old. I'm not the only man who will never see his wife and child again, never work his job, never move freely in the world, but when I think of it, I can't breathe. It feels like a giant hand has a grip on my heart and lungs, crushing the life out of them.

You're the only person I know how to get a letter to, as you're the only member of my family with access to Malchonov, who travels between the frontlines and Moscow. If you have any news, I beg that you share it with me. Anything at all.

Your brother,
Sergei

16.5.44
Vitebsk

Oh Yulia, such a letter! Sergei seems so sad, so different! He's been cowed by prison. To be honest, I feel more softly toward him after reading this than I have in a long time, maybe ever. I'd like to help him, I really would, but Blokhin won't let me go for another six weeks.

And so, the head of the NKVD is a monster, and Sergei's on trial not for crimes he committed, but crimes he refused to commit. I want to tell him that he's right. I want to thank him for not sacrificing Maria to that filth. How hard that he would have to make that choice! To choose between protecting his love, doing what's right, and his life!

My God, these are dangerous thoughts to put to paper. I must not share them with anyone, must not share the dangerous position that Sergei has foisted upon me with anyone else.

How sad that Sergei found the courage to stand up only when his own Maria was threatened. How could he have done that to the others, the girls he didn't know?

I'd gone into the woods to read this letter, and had trouble composing myself enough to come back before the sun went down. I'd agreed to meet Misha at the field kitchen, as I'd done every night for the past three weeks, and I was determined to keep my word and appear as normal as possible. No one can know about these letters, shoved deep into my rucksack.

Misha was waiting for me at the place where we always meet, and saw immediately that something was wrong, that I'd been crying. "What's wrong," he wanted to know, but I just shook my head and forced a smile. He didn't push, instead he tried to cheer me up.

"Hold out your hand," he said, and dropped a candy into it, wrapped in bright orange paper.

You know I love sweets, and I loved that he saved this treat for me, rather than eat it himself. I unwrapped it at once and popped it into my mouth. "Excellent work, Sergeant Panarin. You deserve a commendation. But where did you get it? Is there more?"

Sadly, there wasn't. He'd been lucky to get it from a gunner who just got here from Lithuania. But this little piece of candy, this small gesture of thoughtfulness, turned my mood. The feeling of doom was still there, but now it was layered with a sweet sugar topping.

There was an all-hands assembly after supper, which Misha and I went to together. We got there on the late side, and smashed up with the crowd in the rear to listen to Blokhin, who was already hollering something through a horn, about a big push, a new offensive next month, with all three fronts key to its success. "We're gonna push those fascist bastards all the way back to Berlin!"

"Ypa!"[27] someone shouted, and soon others followed, and it was chaos, with shouts of 'Destroy the Enemy!" The thrill of it rushed through me, and I let out a loud, clear whistle. Misha laughed and tried to whistle too, but it was a pitiful attempt. Yulia, he can't whistle! So funny.

Blokhin motioned for quiet from the podium.

"The war has turned our way, comrades. Now we take our revenge on the savages who tried to stomp us out of existence!"

Hundreds of fists pounded the air, with a deafening roar of cheers.

"Now we exterminate the beasts who burned our villages, who murdered our women and children!"

Yes! My heart was in my ears. "Destroy the enemy!"

The Anthem began to play over the loudspeaker, and everyone began to sing with spirit—thousands of voices united in purpose.

> *Banner of the Soviets, Banner of the people,*
> *May it lead from victory to victory!*

---

27 *Ypa*—Russian for "hurrah!."

We will sweep the vile invaders out of the way!
We shall in battle decide the fate of generations,
We shall lead to glory our Fatherland!

I added my shaky voice to the swell, but had to stop when the tears came back and my throat closed up. Misha sang loud and clear, holding my waist tightly. I hid my face in his neck, hating my weakness.

When the Anthem ended, the crowd split up, floating on dreams of vengeance and glory, while Misha and I walked toward his gun, hand in hand.

Misha, seeing how I was wearing my emotions thinly, asked again if I was all right. I couldn't tell Misha about Sergei's letter. I *wouldn't* tell him. Why put him in danger? "I'm fine," I said, "only wondering if the restrictions on female soldiers will be lifted for the new offensive."

Misha could believe that easily, having heard me complain endlessly about not having anything useful to do. He said he'd been thinking about the "no females in combat" rule and had a new way of looking at it.

"Is it really a crime to go to the Front?" he asked. "Aren't we soldiers at war? Would anyone mind if you just went, Roza?"

I stopped walking and stared at him. "Go to the Front without orders?"

He nodded, and pulled me forward to keep walking, saying that he didn't think anyone would care to pay attention to the actions of one soldier, and was I really bothered about following rules?

You know I've never been one to do as I'm told, and now apparently Misha understands this as well. This makes me so happy, the idea that he's beginning to really know me! And maybe he's right, maybe it would be fine to go on my own, but it's not a decision to make lightly. I need to think about it.

Misha calls his gun "Ferdinand," after the German light-tank. When he first told me of this, I asked him why the devil he would name anything after an enemy weapon? "Irony," he said. Ha! So strange.

We stayed up late, talking, warm and cozy inside Ferdinand's cab, with no talk of Sergei or anything related to the war, just enjoying each other. Unfortunately, I missed curfew and didn't want to face one-and-a-half-Ivans, so I stayed with Misha until just before first light, and went straight to the trench from Ferdinand.

I don't feel guilty about Misha. Mama would warn me off, I know, but I need something to look forward to, a reason to keep going, you know? Everybody does, human nature and all that, and maybe this is even more true for soldiers at war. So much darkness here, and everything written on water. Fyodor and Mikhail dead, and now Sergei in such trouble. I have every reason to be here, to defend the Motherland, to seek vengeance for my brothers, but I also have doubts. Sometimes I wonder if we're the good guys or the bad guys, if I'll ever know the real truth of things. It's all so real but also heavy, like an extra trunk I must drag along with me everywhere, except the weight lives in my heart and the pit of my stomach. Misha and Sasha and Kali—we help each other forget the heaviness. That is the true boon of friendship. I'm sorry Mama doesn't know this.

Now I've written a river and covered several pages of my new journal. I'll stop now. I am kissing you!

19.5.44 May
Sniper quarters

Got new orders last night, finally. I thought *hurrah!* because I don't think I could get through one more evening of forcing smiles and cheerfulness while Misha tells me about his adventures in combat, when the most interesting event of my day was cleaning *Zhanna*. The orders aren't real work, just keeping watch for the *Katyushniks*, the guys who work the *Katyushas*.[28] But maybe we'll get to do some reconnaissance.

You must have heard the *Katyusha* song, it's all over the radio around here, about a woman who waits faithfully at home while her man is fighting on the frontlines. Everyone loves this song, and I like it too. It has a good spirit, and a good tune, but so old-fashioned! Who sits home and waits for her man? And what does a rocket launcher have to do with a woman sitting at home, waiting for her man? But the rocket launchers all have a "K" stamped on them, and the song makes the guys happy, so they started calling them *Katyushas* and it stuck. We aren't allowed to know the real name, you know, for fear someone might put it in a letter that gets past the censors.

Blokhin said Operation Bagration begins in June. I really hope women are allowed back into action by then, or I might take Misha's advice and fight anyway. At the beginning of September I'll be eligible for leave and I hope to go to Yedma. I just hope it's not too late.

---

28 The *Katyushas* (BM-13s) were Soviet WWII rocket launchers known for their ability to pummel the enemy and move away quickly. The Germans called them "Stalin's Organ" due to the eerie sound they made as they flew through the air.

30.5.44

Pyotor Malchonov showed up today, at the billet, and I gave him a letter to give Sergei, but it was a nothing-letter. I'm afraid to write down anything important. What if it's intercepted? Imagine how much trouble I'd be in if the wrong person read that note! I could only write a little news about my life at the Front, and what you have written to me about life in Yedma. But at least it's something for him to read.

Seeing Pyotr, handing him my letter, it occurred to me that he knows *everyone*, and might know who to talk to about getting around the order that restricts females from combat. But when I asked, he gave me a dark look and told me the Red Army had been considering getting rid of the girl snipers entirely! "What the devil," I exclaimed, and he said he'd heard it talked about last month, but since nothing had happened, maybe they changed their minds.

I demanded to know how we could be so disrespected, when we'd gunned down thousands of fascists? Pyotr didn't think it was an issue of respect, just that so many girl snipers have been crushed in the trenches by German tanks. "It's not popular."

This was very hard to hear, and my feelings launched me out of my chair and had me pacing around the table. "So they put men in the trenches to be crushed in our place, while we stay home and warm their beds?"

Pyotr cringed at my anger, said there was some truth to what I was saying, but "Don't blame me, it wasn't my idea."

No, it wasn't Pyotr's doing. He's a friend, he's on our side, Yulia. I sat down again and forced myself to open up, to speak my truth with Pyotr. I told him how much I resented being treated differently than the male soldiers, how much I wanted to be allowed to fight. My voice shook as I spoke, and I was close to tears, but I didn't let myself feel ashamed. "Can you help, Pyotr?"

"Oh, certainly, Roza," he said dryly. "I will go to Chernovosky himself and question his decision to keep the female soldiers safe."

"Really?"

"No!" he barked. Sighed and shook his head, said he couldn't possibly, that he was fond of living and not eager to give it up.

I did cry then, so overwhelmed by my lack of control over my own life. I know life isn't fair, and especially war isn't fair, but I've always had the attitude that with enough determination, I can get what I want. When Papa told me to "obey him or get out," I left and found a better life. This has always been my way, and it's worked for me until now. When I signed up to be a soldier, I signed up to obey absolutely, but I can't stop myself from questioning orders. Why do I have this rebellious nature? It may have served a purpose in the past, but now I need something different.

"There's no harm in being a soldier who wants to fight," Pyotr was saying, sounding remarkably like Misha. "If you are so eager to join your crushed comrades, go and speak with Degtyarev. No one will blame you for asking."

Comrade Major Degtyarev! Maybe he would help me. He showed me respect at Kozie Gory, and put me forward for the Medal of Glory. He would know that I deserve to be allowed to fight!

I'm fond of Pyotr Malchonov, and I think Misha would like him too. I'd like for them to meet, but Misha wasn't enthusiastic when I mentioned it over supper. He just shrugged and asked what was so special about this newspaperman that he would want to meet him? He wasn't impressed when I said Pyotr is very smart, that he knows so many people, and has been so many places, and when I mentioned that everything he writes is read by thousands, Misha said—"You can write about life, or live it," in a brusque-like way.

It was strange that Misha resisted meeting Pyotr. He likes most people, and knows how to talk and charm much better than I do, and Pyotr seemed to me exactly the sort of person who Misha might especially like. I was confused, then a new thought occurred to me. "Are you jealous?"

He recoiled and frowned at me. "Not jealous! But what am I supposed to think when you go on about how amazing he is?"

He was jealous, Yulia! Here was a fun and interesting surprise, and I couldn't help laughing, which made Misha so angry that he got up to leave.

"Pyotr does have beautiful blue eyes," I sighed, leaning back on my elbows, batting my eyelashes.

He glared at me and stalked off.

I called after him, scrambling up to follow. "You have nothing to worry about," I said. "Pyotr is nothing to me next to you."

When he didn't react, I told him I was certain that Pyotr isn't interested in me as a woman. Misha snorted and dismissed that idea, so I shared with him that one afternoon I walked in on Pyotr with his photographer, holding hands and kissing under a tree in a secluded nook of the forest.

Misha slowed his pace and allowed me to fall into step next to him. He was thoughtful for a minute, and then—"Maybe I *should* meet him. He might like me better than you." He winked and gave me his horse grin, showing me all of his teeth, as he often does when he's teasing.

"You have nothing to worry about," he continued. "He's nothing to me next to you—"

"Oh shut up," I said, and that was the end of it. But I think Misha will be open to meeting Pyotr now.

With the sun not yet set, we went by the *Katyushniks* to hear their accordion player and have a glass of vodka. So good to hear music! But our little brother has a greater talent, Yulia.

◈

2.6.44

What can I say about Misha? I can tell you that I love him, really and truly. I know it's only been a few weeks, but he understands me in a way that no one else does. It's like we're on the same level, you know? And when he kisses me, everything else in the world ceases to exist. And I know that he loves me too. There are few things I really believe to be true, but I know that Misha loves me.

I seem to feel everything times ten these days — flying high one minute and flat on the ground the next. I don't feel like I'm under a lot of pressure, but maybe I am and just hide it away. We need to keep our heads clear out here, need to stay distanced from the death and violence, from what we see others do and what we do ourselves. It's a lot to carry, and where does all that boxed up feeling go? For me, it goes to Misha. I'm so grateful to have him, but also worried. I'm too raw, too full of feeling for him. Because what if something happens?

Don't borrow trouble.

10.6.44

I'd like to be a better person, a better comrade to the Motherland. To think of Sergei less often, and worry less about his situation, or about what happened to those Polish prisoners. To never think of that monster Beria. I'd like to have full faith in my government, and in our future as a successful Communist nation. I believe in Stalin, I want to anyway, and I want to believe that the steps we're taking are needed, that I am needed. I struggle for these things, every day.

All of this inaction breeds too much thinking. I'm constantly aware that someone might find this journal, that it could land me in trouble, or worse, bring trouble to my family. But if I can't write about life, how can I understand it? Maybe it's not important for me to understand, in the big picture, but how can I smother the instinct that drives me to understand? I don't think it's possible.

I don't want to become an Enemy of the People and disappear into Siberia. I don't want my family to come to trouble through me. If something happened to you, Yulia, I'd be desperate. But what I really want is the Truth. And I won't be ruled by fear.

Sometimes, I wonder who am I, really, and *what* am I? A soldier who fights for the future of her country, or a puppet on strings? Is it possible to be both at the same time?

I'd like to think only for the collective, to support the good of all, but I can't shut off the other thoughts. Like Sergei, I can't see the good in making sacrifices that feed something evil. Is this the right way of thinking, or do I take myself too seriously?

No one talks about such things, but I did talk to Misha about Sergei. I had to. His latest letter from Lubyanka has weighed on me every second since I got it—the problem of what to do with it rattles around in my brain constantly. I'd decided I would never show either letter to anyone, and then I showed both to Misha, because I thought I would burst from the weight of it, and I thought Misha would want me to share it with him. And, he's a smart guy. Maybe he'd have an idea.

The best place for a private conversation was Ferdinand's cab, which fits only two people, and Misha agreed instantly when I suggested we go there after supper. He probably thought I had something else in mind, as this is where we've spent almost all of our private time, but he entered the conversation enthusiastically enough, and read both of Sergei's letters closely.

"*Oy Daaa,*" Misha said when he finished reading, and asked me how I'd gotten it.

I told him how the first letter had come to me as I boarded the train to begin my tour of duty, and that the second was delivered by Malchonov last week.

Misha nodded and sat lost in thought for a minute or so, and then had a mini burst of anger toward Pyotr. "He shouldn't have done it."

"It's not like he knew what was in the letter," I said, which I'm sure is true, because both letters were sealed.

"Let me keep them," he suggested, and I froze, a seed of dread blossoming in my stomach. What would he do with them? Was I wrong to trust him? I looked at him cautiously, wondering *Who is this man?*

"Oy, such a look!" he said with a laugh. "But really, Roza, don't you know how much trouble you'll be in if you're caught with those letters?"

Oh, I knew. I'd imagined all kinds of dark happenings, but there was no way I was going to hand over the burden to him, who had nothing to do with Sergei or anyone at Yedma. "Do you seriously think I'm going to give you those letters?"

"Why not? No one's going to search *my* stuff."

"I'm not giving them to you."

"So stubborn," he frowned. "What if I insist?"

"If you *insist*?" I repeated, sitting straight up on the edge of my seat.

"I'm not important," he said loudly. "I don't have my picture in the papers, I don't have command of a platoon. They'll will be safer with me."

"I'm not going to be the one who gets you killed," I yelled, "and you're not the boss of me!"

Misha shoved the letters in his breast pocket and crossed his arms stubbornly over his chest. Here it was again, the *let's-take-care-of-the-weak-females* way of thinking, and from Misha!

"You think I'm weak!"

"No," he said, with an emphatic shake of his head. "You're not weak, just stubborn. Too stubborn to see the truth in what I'm saying."

I lunged at his pocket to get back my letters, but he was ready for me. We had a bit of a tussle, less fun than other wrestling matches we've had in Ferdinand, but anger lent me super strength and I ended up with them.

I threw open the door and leapt out, clutching Sergei's letters, relieved to have the onerous things back in my possession. I stopped for half a second to glare at Misha, thinking it might be the last time I looked the bastard in the face, and turned to flee.

Misha called after me, in a peace-seeking manner, but I ran and ran, not willing to hear whatever excuses he'd make up to get the letters away from me.

I should have trusted my first instinct and not shown him. Now he knows I have them, and I don't think he'd use that against me, but he's not on my side in what needs to be done. He's not going to help me figure out how to get the letters to Papa. And now I've lost Misha. I don't think I'll ever look at him the same way, knowing he's just like all the other men who try to control me. He *insists* that he keep them! God and Hell! How could he think for one instant that I'd let him, or anyone, take those letters away from me? To the devil with Mikhail Panarin.

12.6.44

A special assignment came in last night, working with the gunners, and the timing was great for me. So glad for something important to do, and something to think about, that doesn't include worrying about Misha and Sergei.

Some of the artillery units have been dogged by a German sniper the past few days. Misha's unit is working further south, so I don't have that worry, but a few units near no-man's land have been stalked by a Fritz sniper for three days, and he has taken down three of our boys. Really sad, although I didn't know those guys, and very scary for the other guys. They're rattled, feeling as if they might be blown away at every instant, and with good cause. Last night, I got word that our platoon was assigned to track the sniper and take him down, and I decided that Lida and I would take on the job. It's been extremely interesting — a whole new level of hunting. Like a really difficult puzzle, with super high stakes. Winner take all — lose, and you're dead. It's the ultimate show down.

I'm grateful and a little amazed that they didn't try to keep the female snipers out of it. This is clearly a job for a sniper, but they could have put male snipers on the job, and they didn't. I expect because the action doesn't take place anywhere near the frontlines. Whatever the reason, I'm glad for it, and glad to be working with Lida again. She's smart, which is important, and we get along very well.

We dropped into the trench near the targeted area before sun up this morning, planning to build a decoy to lure the Fritz sniper into shooting at us and exposing his position. We suspected that he was shooting from a thatch of trees on the far eastern edge of the field, quite a bit lower than our trench, but we had to find his exact position if we were going to take him down. That meant we needed him to shoot, so that we could see where he was hiding.

We wanted something better than the standard trench decoy, which involves attaching a helmet to the end of a stick and moving it up and down near the edge of the trench. Every sniper in the world knows that trick, and it only ever works on a sniper who is very inexperienced or very far away. And likely this Fritz was far away, but who knew? We needed something better, because if the sniper spotted the decoy, he would move and we would never get him. Lida had brought along a lot of extra clothes and things with her to the trench, so we set to work building a well-disguised decoy.

Decoys can be fancy. Once, I saw a dummy that looked like an officer having a smoke, with strings attached to the arms to puppet him around. Seems like it might be fun to build something like that, but not necessary in this case, where the sniper's hide was distant, and it would take too much time. We needed to get the job done fast so we didn't lose any more of our guys. We decided that the best plan was to build a reasonable looking dummy from the neck up, so we shoved clothes inside a bread bag to form a round face, and Lida scraped out some eyes with a charred piece of wood. Then we needed only to slap a half-camouflaged helmet on its head, shove a stick through it to act like a handle, tape the whole thing together with some miracle stuff from the Americans called "duck tape", and our dummy was ready.

I propped him against the trench wall and we sat back to admire our handiwork.

"Let's call him Feliks, for luck," Lida said.

That seemed a splendid idea. All our hopes were resting on Feliks, on his ability to lure the Fritz sniper into shooting at him. We could use all the luck we could get.

We know that German snipers most often carry a Mauser 98K, whose round is slightly wider than our Mosin's, with about the same range. There's no way to know for sure that this Fritz was using a 98K, but it didn't really matter, since most German sniper rifles use the same ammo, with similar range. Since the sniper had been settled into his hide for a few days in a row, it was safe to assume that he was at the far end of his range, where we wouldn't hear his weapon fire. So, 400–500 meters away, in the eastern forest.

I'd be lying if I said I was really confident about our assessment. There's no way to be sure that this Fritz didn't have a completely different weapon, and wasn't positioned somewhere else entirely. But there was a good chance we were right. What else could we do, but trust ourselves?

It was halfway through the morning when we finished our decoy and talked through where the sniper was probably hiding. The next step was for me to climb a tree or get into some other high position where I had a good view of the eastern woods, while Lida stayed in the trench and dipped the dummy above and below the trench line every hour, on the hour, to lure the sniper into shooting, while I watched like a hawk for a muzzle flash or any kind of movement. At least, that was the plan I had in mind. Lida was thinking something else.

"I can take the shot, Roza," she said, as I was scanning the area with my binoculars to find a good roosting spot.

I stopped scouting and looked at her in surprise. It never occurred to be that Lida could be shooter, with me working the dummy. I had always planned on doing the shooting myself.

To be fair, Lida is a good sharp shooter. Very good. She could probably pull off that shot. I guess we both wanted it, but I was convinced that I should be the one to do it. I have a higher kill count, with more difficult kills. And the assignment had come to me, as commander of the platoon. Did she really think that I'd brought her along to shoot, rather than assist?

I didn't want to say outright that I was a better shot than Lida, although I think it might be true. Instead, I said that we'd have a better chance of getting the sniper with me shooting, rather than her, because I had more experience.

"Roza, you and I were deployed on the exact same day, and have been out here the exact same amount of time," she said, hands on her hips.

And that was true, but I had done more to prove myself than she had since we were deployed. And I really believed that I was the better one to take this shot. Maybe Lida could do the job, but I didn't know that for sure. I've never seen her shoot at distance.

"But I have more experience with long-range targets," I said.

"I don't know. I've hit targets from really far away," she said, a bit icily. "And I'm an excellent spotter, even you must admit that."

I didn't know what to say to that, so I said nothing.

"Roza," she continued, "it would be really great if you'd let someone else get some glory for a change. You've had so many chances to prove yourself, and I haven't. Let it be my turn. I know I can do it!"

This was so hard for me, Yulia, not only because I didn't like hearing that I might be perceived as a glory hog, but because I knew in my heart that I was the one who would take the shot — not Lida. I didn't need to consider it. Lida might be a great sniper, and a great spotter, and I might admire her ambition, and wish her all of the shooting opportunities in the world, but getting this Fritz sniper was serious business and I wasn't going to hand over control to Lida just because she asked.

But I did try hard to be nice when I told her that I had chosen her to come with me to assist, not to shoot, and that I wanted to keep things that way. I had the authority, and she had no choice but to accept my words, but it didn't make her happy.

"I could get that shot," she muttered, and sat down heavily on the trench floor, arms crossed tightly across her body, with her head turned away from me.

The gunner's trench was designed with a healthy downward slope out the back, so it was pretty safe for me to belly crawl out and make my way over to the tree I'd picked out. From there, things got riskier, because it was daylight, and I could be spotted. I stood flush against the tree on the side that should be hidden from the Fritz sniper's view, summoning the nerve to begin the climb, when it occurred to me that he wasn't likely to be watching the trees—he was targeting the gunners, and they were on the ground. I wasn't sure I was right, but the thought gave me the courage to shimmy up the trunk, slowly and carefully, my heart pounding, expecting to be shot at every moment. I reached my perch safely, when the sun was directly overhead.

Lida watched for the moment when I got into position before she started running the decoy, and for the next several hours, which seemed like weeks, we flirted with the Fritz sniper, with Lida pushing the helmet just above the wall and moving it around to make it look like a real soldier. Every hour on the hour. This was trickier than it sounds, because not only did the movements need to look natural, but the helmet needed to be positioned straight up and down, so that we could get accurate measurements of the angle of impact, in case we needed to resort to ballistics to find the shooter. Meanwhile, I was lying flat on my stomach on a particularly large Y branch of my tree, with Zhana under my stomach, pointed in the direction of the enemy. Each time that I saw Lida start up with the decoy, I would comb the woods with my naked eyes, binoculars poised for use if I saw anything suspicious. We carried on doing this forever, without any action from the sniper. It was exhausting, and also worrying. What would our next step be if he didn't go for the decoy?

Patience is always hard for me to find, and waiting for that sniper today was excruciating. But eventually, just as the sun was close to setting, he took the bait, and *Bam!* I heard a round hit our decoy's helmet. My eyes, and my intuition, wide open and trained on the enemy woods, had taken in some slight movement a moment before impact, and I trained my binoculars on that section of the landscape. I immediately focused in on a big tree that seemed like the right place to me. It was the only tree that looked like a good long-term perch for a sniper. I felt certain he was there, in that tree, and watched it without blinking.

But it wasn't enough to strongly suspect that the sniper was in that tree. To get a clean shot, I needed to see his body clearly, to aim to kill, and witness his death. And I needed to stay invisible while doing it. If my shot didn't hit the mark, he would retaliate, either at me, or at Lida in the trench. A shot on the sniper's ear or the hand would be no good, and might get one of us killed.

When the sun began to set in earnest, the tree I was watching became backlit with bright orange and yellow, and suddenly I could see him, the Fritz. Or rather, I saw a dark bump in the tree, that didn't look like part of the tree. It was the sniper's silhouette! His body was melded to the trunk, and I didn't have a clean shot on it, but I could see his helmet, outlined so clearly in bright orange. I could get him by shooting the helmet. Carefully, so carefully, adjusting for distance, the downward slope, and the light breeze, I aimed my rifle and squeezed the trigger. And I got him, Yulia. The helmet snapped back and the sniper fell from his perch, striking against the tree's limbs on the way down. I couldn't see him after he fell to the ground — it was too far away. But I definitely got him, and I heard Lida cheer like crazy from the trench.

Back at camp, everyone knew that we got the sniper today, and the gunners treated me like a celebrity. "Our hero!" said Toska, Sasha's boyfriend, and I felt myself blush.

"And Lida," I said, grabbing her arm and pulling her next to me. I really did want her to share in the glory. "It would not have been possible without Lida. She was with me on everything."

I am proud, Yulia, and humbled. It must be the dream of every sniper, to take down an enemy sniper. It's said to be a mark of greatness. I'm relieved I was able to do it, because I wasn't sure. I wondered what Misha would think, but didn't see him anywhere. I don't think he was at dinner. It would have been nice for him to witness my victory, for him to see that I'm not weak, but strong. That I'm busy working, and not thinking about him, about his betrayal.

15.6.44
Still near Vitebsk, lying on our stomachs all day

It was great to get the German sniper, but now we're back to doing nothing. I want so badly to go to the frontlines. Or anywhere, really. I'd do anything to get my mind off Misha and Sergei, to get away from this blackness that comes over me when I'm forced to sit on my hands. Early this morning, I caught a lift to headquarters to speak with Major Degtyarev to ask for permission to go forward. I waited two hours to see him, but he brushed me off like a fly. "It'd be a direct violation of my orders to send you to the Front."

I cried a little on the ride back to the billet. Degtyarev was my last hope. What is wrong with the world that I, a decorated soldier, assigned a position as Senior Sergeant in command of a sniper platoon, cannot get permission to shoot my gun at the enemy? Everyone keeps telling me I should be grateful to be safe. Gratitude is not what I'm feeling.

And Misha. He approached at supper, tried to join our *troika* with a pretense that everything was normal. After ignoring me all week, Yulia! Sasha and Kali kept looking back and forth between us when I didn't greet him and tried to ignore him.

"Roza's mad at me," he told them.

"What did you do?" Sasha asked.

"Nothing she wouldn't have done," he said, and when I glared at him, added—"It's a private matter."

I wanted to speak up, to let my friends know it wasn't *that* kind of private matter, but I couldn't tell them about the letter, so what could I say? And what did Misha think he was doing, driving right into the argument without caring that I was sitting with my friends in the middle of the field kitchen? I jerked my head toward Sasha and Kali, but he just sat there calmly, looking at me.

"Is it a crime to wish to keep you safe?"

God and Hell, Misha really didn't care about keeping my secret! I leapt to my feet, grabbed him by the arm, dragged him away from my friends and asked him what on earth he thought he was doing. It turns out he deliberately approached me when I was with my friends, thinking that I would just walk away from him if he came to me alone, and I probably would have, Yulia, but this was also completely unacceptable! Did he need to speak with me so badly that he was willing to put my friends in danger?

"They'll press me to know what's going on!" I said, practically hissing at him.

He insisted that they wouldn't, if I told them it was safer not to know. "They're smart girls."

True. Sasha and Kali haven't spent their life in a tree. In some ways, they're smarter than I am. But it seemed an unnecessary risk, and I told him so.

"Don't turn this into a problem," Misha said. "The real issue is what you're carrying."

I began to argue that I wasn't carrying anything, because I'd hidden the letters deep inside my things at the billet, but stopped half-way through, worried he might try to steal them, if he knew where to look. His face grew grim as I talked, his mouth hardening into a thin line.

I asked him if he really wanted to fight about this again. Hadn't he heard me when I said he wasn't my boss? Didn't he understand that I don't want him to protect me, as if I was some helpless little girl?

Misha rolled his shoulders and took a deep breath. No, he didn't want to fight, he just wanted to ask me a question, and he wanted me to really listen. I looked at him, his face so serious, his body taut. I could see that he was trying, that he wanted to be calm, but his eyes were storm clouds, his nostrils flared, his shoulders tensed. So handsome, my Misha, even when he's mad.

"How did things get so messed up?" I wondered, and must have said it aloud, because he blinked and softened a little bit.

"I want to know what you would do if our situations were reversed," Misha said.

At first, I thought he meant what would I do if I was a man and he was a woman, but no, he meant if he was carrying a document that disclosed heinous crimes perpetrated by one of the most powerful men in the country, and "had no plan to get rid of it," what would I do?

I would do whatever he wanted me to do, and that's just what I said. I don't think he believed me, because he grabbed my arms, looked me straight in the eyes and accused me of trying to manipulate him with that answer. Then he asked again, what would I do?

But I didn't have another answer, I really do think that I would respect his wishes.

He dropped his hands and looked at me with deep frustration. "You'd try to get those letters from me. You'd consider it a noble act, and take all of the risk onto yourself to spare me," he said.

Now *I* was mad, and told him it was rude to tell me what I thought. Was he inside my head, reading my thoughts? Does he think he knows me better than I know myself?

He said maybe he did, because it was clear to him that I care nothing for my own life, that I'm eager to throw myself in the way of death, to save him, or Sergei, or "the company dog."

He spat the words out in anger, meant them as a judgment against me, but I didn't hear anything insulting in what he said, only in the way he was speaking to me.

"Am I supposed to apologize for being brave, for not putting myself before others?" I asked.

"That's not the same as looking for reasons to die!"

This was going too far. I've never tried to die, Yulia. There is something at work, something I don't fully understand, that keeps me calm in combat, and makes it easy for me to put myself in danger, but that doesn't mean I want to die. But I was too offended to take the trouble to explain.

Misha sighed. "Just think about it," he said, and spun away.

My body lurched after him, wanting to follow, wanting to erase all this arguing and go back to the way things have been between us for the past month, but my feet stayed rooted to the ground.

Writing now, I can't stop crying. What was I supposed to do? What exactly does Misha want me to think about? I don't need to mull over whether or not Sergei's letters are a dangerous possession, don't need to wonder whether or not I'm willing to put Misha at risk for my own family business. I know my own truth here — he's not dying for Sergei or me, or some old-fashioned idea of chivalry. Why does he have to act the brave warrior protecting the weak damsel? *Infuriating.* Same old *men strong women weak* that we grew up on, but I really thought he saw me as an equal. I'm so disappointed, and Sad. Sad sad sad. I thought I understood the way things were between us, but maybe I just saw what I wanted to see.

16.6.44

But you, wild rover, pray for tempests,
As if in tempests there were peace!

This, from Lermontov, keeps running through my mind. How well he puts it—the urge to be in the middle of the action. That is me.

"It's not a crime to go to the Front. No one will look for you," Misha had said, maybe two weeks ago, when we were still together, still speaking. And now, Yulia, I'm fading away, with no Misha and no interesting work. I wish I could be happy doing support for the *Katyushniks*, but my feet are itchy. It's not that I'm eager to die, like Misha thinks, and I'm not looking for glory. Something else, an invisible hand, pushes me into the thick of the fight.

Fedya came to me again last night, in a dream. He looked perfect this time, no gaping hole in his chest, his face washed smooth with peacefulness. He didn't say a single word but I felt like he was giving me permission to go, to live life on my own terms. I woke up determined to steal away to the frontlines, and left almost instantly, only taking time to wrap my feet and shove this journal into my rucksack.

I slunk away through the woods and swamps, wearing camouflage. As I got closer to the sounds of mortar blasts, the air was thick with gray dust in every direction; on the trees, on my suit and in my hair, suspended in the air itself so that the light from the rising sun was strangled, and could only burst through in thin rays. I couldn't see where I was going, and heard German spoken all around, so I crept by inches, not making a sound, my heart beating in my ears. Then I heard Russian to my right, to the north, so I headed that way and found the 1136th Artillery Regiment. I didn't know these guys, but they accepted me as one of their own, shared their breakfast, and invited me to go on patrol with a group of them to clear the Nazis out of an area in the woods.

We were just heading out when I got a note from Blokhin. "Go back to your platoon," it said, nothing more.

Damn that Blokhin! How did he find me so soon? Who was the rat who told on me? I couldn't disobey a direct order, so I headed back toward the rear, buzzing with frustration.

As the distance between myself and the fighting grew wider, my mind wandered to Sergei and his last wretched letter, and Misha. My constant obsessions. *What if I insisted?* he'd said. To protect me. But if he was really trying to protect me, why encourage me to go to the Front? Smells like a lie, Yulia. Why did he really want the letters? To use against me? Misha's not like that.

I kicked these thoughts along and onto a bridge, when I happened to look down and saw some Fritz huddled on the river bank beneath. Everything in my head ran away, the world shifted, and I was, again, not just a girl, but a soldier. Even my skin seemed to get tougher, a battle hide, and all of the scenery and sounds of the forest became gray and dull, as if they'd agreed to fade away to provide me with an easy way to track the enemy.

I whipped my rifle off my back and cocked it, prepared to take him out at the slightest sign of a fight. "*Hände hoch*,"[29] I shouted.

Six hands went into the air. Three men, then. I could handle them. One kept jabbering in German, I thought he was asking a question but I didn't understand. Never learned much German.

"Up here now!" I yelled, gesturing with my rifle. All three crawled up the bank and I confiscated their grenades, binoculars, watches, and a very nice *finka*,[30] which I stuck immediately into my belt. I

---

29 *Hände hoch*—German for "hands up."
30 A *finka* is traditionally a Finnish combat knife, and generally meant something like "bad ass knife" to the Soviets during WWII.

noticed that their uniforms were in rags, and they had just one gun between them. I thought the Germans were powerful, well-armed, but here was the opposite, here was proof that Fritz is suffering, that we are winning the war.

I pushed the Germans 1.5 km to headquarters, with their hands on their heads, and entered the village marching down the center of the road, my rifle to the backs of the fascists, my head held high, the *finka* shining on my belt. When I reached the inn, everyone came out from dinner and cheered like crazy to see that I had three prisoners under my power. In that moment, I was *sto*,[31] Yulia. A true warrior. I, alone, had brought in three full-grown German prisoners.

Blokhin was there, at the inn, and invited me to join him and some other brass for dinner. There was milk, which tasted so good that I almost cried, and pork, and soup with dumplings, and then a sweet honey custard. Whenever I caught Blokhin's eye, he frowned at me, and at one point he leaned over and said "We need to talk." But he wouldn't chastise me in front of the group, when so many were singing my praises. But I couldn't resist reminding him that I was on my way back to the rear when I came upon the Germans, that I'd been following his orders.

Back home, I was reprimanded for leaving my unit, and told that the *Komsomol* had put me on watch. I was also told that I'd be put forward for a second Order of Glory for capturing an enemy officer, because one of my prisoners turned out to be an officer. So, what am I to think, having been both punished and rewarded for my little adventure away from the platoon?

---

31 *Sto*—Russian slang for "bad ass."

17.6.44

Sasha and Kali confronted me over breakfast—not the best start to a new day. I saw right away that they'd planned this ahead of time, because they practically pounced on me as soon as I sat down and they were together on everything. What's going on with Misha? Why did I leave to go to the Front? Wasn't I supposed to be commanding the platoon? I felt so attacked, I could hardly swallow my *kasha*. I trust Sasha and Kali more than anyone, but look what happened when I showed Misha Sergei's letters! What if I told them and it broke up our *troika?*[32]

"I can't tell you about Misha," I said, with that hateful whine I sometimes get in my voice. "You have to trust me on this."

They looked at each other and agreed, reluctantly, to drop it, but still pushed to know why I had run away to the Front. I could only respond with an explosion of anger over the Red Army's policies.

"But we have to follow orders," Kali said.

It occurred to me to point out that I was her superior in command. Instead, I told them that in defying orders, I'd been put forward for another Order of Glory, so who was to say that what I did was wrong?

Kali couldn't mask her surprise over this news, and immediately veered the conversation into a discussion about the relativity of "right" and "wrong." Echoes of our conversation over breakfast at Kozy Gorie, but now I understood more clearly what she'd meant back then, and I wasn't so quick to disagree. And isn't it interesting that her irritation over me leaving the platoon evaporated when she learned about the medal?

---

32 *Troika*—Russian for "trio."

Sasha wasn't so easily appeased, and set herself toward persuading me to stay with the platoon and support the *Katyushniks*, "because we'll go back into the trenches soon enough anyway."

I tried not to be annoyed with Sasha telling me what to do. I'm sure she means well, and it's not her fault I have this problem with authority. I didn't agree or disagree, but I do feel bad about leaving the platoon. I don't want to be a bad commander, and don't want any of the snipers to think badly of me, but the platoon doesn't need to be told how to sit on their hands and wait for real orders!

I stayed close to the girls today, and went with them to bathe in the lake. The sun was hot and everyone was cheerful—we sang as we marched down the hill, "The Germans stamped their feet, darning their rags." I was content in the moment, and wondered if it wouldn't be all right to stay in the rear with the platoon.

The water felt like home—very cold. Such a feeling, jumping into the icy lake! I scrubbed myself pink, then dove beneath the surface, then floated, when suddenly there came a loud whooping and a pack of naked men rushed the lake! We screamed to wake the dead when they splashed into the water and grabbed at us.

One of them got Sasha, and she squealed and kicked, laughing, but Kali sprinted out immediately and ducked into the woods. "Shame on you!" she shouted, a loud, clear voice from behind a tree.

Someone's arms came around me from behind and lifted me off the bottom. I elbowed him in the chest, hard, and he dropped me, sending me under. I came up spitting water, mad as a wild hen, and another boy seized me. *Mudak!* I thrashed to be free and slugged at his jaw, but slid on the slick mud and barely brushed his shoulder, then I jumped up the slippery bank before someone else could get hold of me.

"Who do you think you are?" I shouted, my heart in my throat, naked as the day I was born.

"Aw, we're just having some fun," one of the scoundrels said.

"Fun for you!" I scolded. "Come on, girls."

But fear had turned them into statues in the water, arms wrapped protectively around themselves. Except for Sasha, who looked comfortable with her arms around her captor's neck.

"Look the other way," I commanded the boys.

There were some whines and complaints, but most of them turned their backs, and the girls came rushing out. The boy who held Sasha looked into her eyes and let her down, reluctantly, before she joined the rest of us by the tree where we'd hung our clothes. We grabbed our things and tore out of there. Sasha, Kali and I ran as a *troika*, and came to a pause in the woods to get dressed.

I shouted off some of my frustration as I tugged on my camouflage. Those stupid boys! Why did they think they could do anything they wanted to us, because we are girls!

But Sasha was not upset with them, she felt they were just "boys being boys," and who wants a weakling?

I experienced a revelation, a flash of understanding, and realized that Sasha wasn't wrong. We want strong men, warriors, but we curse them for their boldness. How difficult, Yulia!

But Kali did NOT agree, and got very stern with Sasha, almost yelling, asking her how she could encourage their behavior. Sasha yelled right back, and they faced-off, hands on hips, shouting at each other.

"They were children, lads at war!" Sasha said. Kali just snorted and said something under her breath about Sasha letting that boy runs his hands over her body as a "service to the Motherland."

Sasha's next words came loudly, each word framed with intensity. "Most of us will die out here. How many of those boys will be dead before the snows come, without ever touching a woman's breast?"

"And so you volunteer."

Sasha threw her hands up in the air and called Kali a stick in the mud. "At least I'm not self-centered," she added, accusingly, which struck me as a low blow.

"Oh sure, you're the angel of selflessness!" Kali said. "Don't you see that you're making it worse? Why don't you understand that the only way to get them to stop treating us like dirt is to resist!"

"Right. I'm the downfall of our entire gender," Sasha said, sounding very offended. She spun around and stalked off in the direction of the billet.

Kali and I followed her at a less emotional pace, with Kali complaining about how horrible those boys were, and how Sasha encouraged it, even enjoyed it. "She can only see what's right in front of her," Kali said, and wondered what Toska would think, because neither he nor Misha would harass a group of women having a bath.

I agreed, they wouldn't. We walked the rest of the way home in silence, my thoughts on Misha. He was kind to me when we were together, almost always. He cared about my comfort, my thoughts, but he's also fierce. He's a strong man. Maybe it's natural to want to protect me from Sergei's letters. Maybe I would have done the same, in his place. Maybe I've borrowed trouble.

You'll have to pay it back, with interest.

Yes, Mama. Maybe I will.

I hate their bickering. Sasha and Kali. They're like sisters, fighting like devils one minute and thick as thieves the next. Except you and I never fought like that. Because we are four years apart? But their argument did teach me something—life flies fast and I want to make it up with Misha. And I think I know how to do it.

14 June 1944
Yedma

To: Senior Sergeant Roza Shanina
Fifth Army, 184th Rifle Division
Dearest Roza,

I hope you're well, and continuing your good work to exterminate the enemy. We hear promising news here, but it's difficult to know the truth of what's happening, isolated as we are, so far from any city or military camp. Pavel has gone to the war, has been deployed into the Second Front.

In your last letter you alluded to some trouble about S. which led Papa to inquire after him, and the lack of information is very troubling — every inquiry is met with silence. Oh, how I long for simpler days! To see you, and have a real conversation over a nice cup of tea. Let us hope it will be a short wait until the time comes when the fascists flee our country.

I confess a terror has taken root in my heart. I try not to feed it, but it wants to be heard. Now it howls like a wolf; now it is crying, like a lost child. I think of you many times throughout the day, and wish you were here with me, but I do not expect it. I will not beg you to come, but will continue to tend the cows, and help Mama however I can, and watch for the mail, while anticipation and fear duel for the higher place in my heart. I do beg you to take care of yourself, and come to us when you can, if only to give your sister a reason to hold hope for the future.

Your Yulia

20.6.44
Vitebsk billet

My Yulia, if only I could visit, I'd be there tomorrow! I long to give you a hug, to have tea with your *medovik*,[33] and to get rid of Sergei's letters. I mean to say, I want to fulfill my duty to him and deliver the letters to Papa, but they are such a giant thorn in my side and I'd love to be done with them. But there's no possibility for leave yet, so no end in sight. We must both carry on.

I kissed the dirt with Misha and we've healed the breach. My plan worked—we reconciled because I decided to let him carry the letters. Just for a time, although I didn't mention that part to him.

"You must promise, Misha, really and truly, that you won't destroy them," I said, and he agreed. And I believe him, Yulia.

Afterwards, after we talked—the way he looked at me! Those grey eyes smiling into me and warming me right down to my toes. In this moment, I understand what happiness is. But I hope I did the right thing. I'll die if he gets caught with the letters.

1.7.44

Misha's been given a week's furlough starting a week from tomorrow, and plans to go home to Moscow. I was worried that he might get noble and try to take the letters to Yedma, or might get searched somewhere in his travels and disappear into Siberia, so I asked him to give me back the letters to hold while he was on leave.

He balked at first, then relented, probably wishing to avoid another argument, so now I'm once again carrying the damned

---

33 *Medovik*—a Russian honey cake.

things. They make me jumpy. Amazing how much power is contained in those two little pieces of paper, folded into a tiny rectangle, that couldn't stop a bullet, but could get me killed. It seems a living thing that wishes me ill.

8.7.44

Misha left this morning, and the week ahead stretches long, like a boring lecture on the price of wheat. What to do with myself?

10.7.44
Somewhere between Vitebsk and Vilnius

Have barely had time for a thought toward Misha, since the entire Third Front has moved forward, 500,000 soldiers and tanks and artillery lumbering across the Lithuanian border like a giant beast. We've left our little farmhouse behind forever and are now camped in tents, sleeping on top of our *plash palatkas*. The lower flank has pushed Fritz all the way back to the Vistula, and knocks on the door of Warsaw. Our battalion pushes north, toward the German Königsberg. But after today's long march, I learned there's no change in my platoon's orders. We are slated to work support for the *Katyushniks* during the Vilnius offensive. This, while the rest of the army is charging the enemy! Tomorrow, I make my break for the Front. I can't bear to graze in a field at the rear when so many battles are taking place. And with Misha gone, what could hold me back?

12.7.44

Left yesterday afternoon, and after a couple of hours of slinking through the woods, I ran into the lead battalion of the 36th rifle division. I went straight to headquarters, to find a place to fight, and ran into Shura and Duce, two snipers I know from the women's rallies. What a relief to see friendly faces! They introduced me to Vanya Horopov, commander of the battalion, who seems a good guy, a decent commander. We took our dinner together and all got along great, but the best part was that Horopov didn't ask for my orders, and Blokhin was nowhere. The battalion was set to attack that same night, last night, and easy as pie, I was to go with Duce and the 36th RD.

We went on the attack at three in the morning, charged forward all at once, fire all around, and I was at the front of combat formations, wreaking destruction with my rifle. It was glorious, Yulia! We took the hill quickly, and dropped into a trench on the berm to prepare for a counter-attack.

Suddenly Blokhin was there, right next to me in the trench, and saw that I was in the thick of it.

He scowled at me. "Come now, little girl, go back to the rear."

Grrrr! How is he everywhere I want to be?

"I'll go back when the battle is over," I said, not quite as firmly as I'd wanted.

He pinned me with black eyes, snorted, and muttered something about getting the commissar to haul me back to the rear. He grabbed the field telephone from his lieutenant, who was at his elbow, and gave the battery crank a spin. "Shapiro? Shapiro! Get down here, you motherfucker!"

I eyed Blokhin with dread when he grinned at me sideways, looking like a cat who'd just got its mouse. He knew he had all the power and I none — he would make me go back to the rear like a good little sheep.

Twenty minutes later, Shapiro had dragged me away from the fight and left me in the woods a couple of kilometers away, with the order to "go home."

I wandered around, frustrated, unsure where to go. I didn't want to go to the rear, and honestly, I wasn't sure how to get there. *Lost and freezing*, I thought, wearing only my bra and panties under camouflage, without even a *telnyashka*[34] for warmth. I needed to keep moving.

Finally, I climbed a tree and scouted around with my binoculars. I could see signs of Fritz to the east, west and south. A guard loomed to the north, but was he ours, or theirs? Too far to tell, so I got down and crept toward him until I saw the green uniform. *Hurrah!* I scurried on my belly through the thick grass and rose to full height directly in front of the guard, and what do you think? He was asleep! Sleeping on his boots, with several infantry guards curled up on the ground around him. I poked him on the shoulder and he almost shot me in surprise. "Who's there?"

I told him who I was, and got a shock when he said he'd heard of me! He'd seen a picture of me in the paper, and seemed happy to see me in the flesh. He was with the 157th, under the command of Nikolai Solomatin, who I've met twice through his friendship with the *Katyushniks*.

Introductions over, the guard yawned and complained that we didn't need to get up for at least a couple more hours. I was gutted with exhaustion and needed no more invitation, so I lied down with the other soldiers and fell into a dead sleep. Not sure how long I was out, but the sun is high in the sky and I've been awake for one hour. I'm so excited to be here, Yulia. This is the forwardmost company

---

34 *Telnyashka* — a warm, blue and white-striped undershirt, standard issue for Red Army soldiers.

at the Front! Except for the *shtrafbat*,³⁵ who always go first. Suicide squads, they are, made up of prisoners. I wouldn't want to go with those guys, but I'm happy to follow in their footsteps.

12.7.44
Solomatin's camp near Vilnius

I had just stowed my journal and was sitting with my back against a tree, pondering my next step, when I heard "Roza Shanina," and found Solomatin looking down at me.

I leapt to my feet and let him know that I'd been separated from my unit, and my rifle was at his service, if he had a place for me to fight. He seemed interested, seemed to be considering the idea, when we were distracted by the whir of a plane engine, and looked up to see a *Luftwaffe*³⁶ fighter strafe the ground 100 meters away, near our artillery line. The Germans were attacking!

Ten minutes later, I found myself in a trench along the berm of the central hill, rifle perched on its edge, waiting for the enemy. I looked down the line at the guard platoon I'd tacked onto, thrilled to be there. Solomatin had not kicked me out, had just rushed away without saying anything. Good as permission, to my thinking.

Two more planes strafed the ground behind us, but our anti-aircraft was ready this time, and got them. Then the ground troops came, troops riding on self-propelled guns, stalking us across the charred field, tanks bringing up the rear. I felt blood racing through

---

35 The *shtrafbat* units were made up of prisoners and those who fell out of favor with the Party. They were scouts who did the most dangerous work along the front lines.

36 *Luftwaffe*—the air combat branch of the German *Wehrmacht* during WWII.

my limbs, and my surroundings came alive, everything outlined in bright white light. This is what I craved. What I needed to feel alive.

Mosinas are built for long-range shooting, so I could shoot *Zhanna* before the others, and I began to take Fritz out, one by one. I shot well, at least ten kills.

The tanks rumbled closer, beasts with metal hide that my bullets could not pierce. One enemy tank came strongly toward the trench just to my left. I took a shot at it, although I knew it wasn't likely to make an impact, and my rifle jammed.

God and Hell, I thought. *Defenseless!* I sank to the bottom of the trench and worked to clear the jam as fast as I could. When I sprang back up, the enemy tank was bearing down hard on the neighboring trench, within six meters of it, and three men leapt out with a battle cry and charged at it, trying to get to the hatch. The massive wheels crushed two of them, rolled right over them as I watched, forced to listen to their screams and the sharp sound of bones cracking. One of them had captain's stripes. The third man, a real hero, got a grenade down the hatch and the whole thing blew up, spitting metal and gore and black smoke for ten meters in every direction, while I hunkered down and covered my head.

Back in position, I saw another tank coming directly toward me, fifteen meters away. I reached for my grenade—gone! Where was it? I eyed the tank, calculating how I could best attack with no grenades. *Zhanna* would be too slow at close range, but my bayonet might be useful. They'd be on me in a minute, I had nothing to lose. I hoisted myself up, ready to run, when the thing blew, and I was thrown back onto the trench floor by the force of it. Still alive.

They were all around, the tanks. Panzers, rocking back and forth on the trenches, or on their way to do so. There was machine gun fire, and mortar shells crashing into metal—a battle symphony that set my ears ringing. But soon, our anti-tank fire increased, and the Panzers began to blow, one after another, as our 76 mms took them out. It was indescribably thrilling, watching those tanks explode. I shouted *"Ypa"* eight times, for eight enemy tanks exploded, and I heard shouts from all the neighboring trenches, who must have been feeling something like what I was feeling. In that moment, I was connected to something bigger than myself. I understood the importance of what we were doing. And for the first time, I felt sure we would succeed, whatever the cost.

When all was quiet, I climbed out of the trench, tripped over a severed leg, still booted, and almost lost the NK ration I'd devoured earlier.

A groan came from somewhere to my left. I turned and saw the captain who'd been crushed, somehow still alive. I crawled over to him, averting my eyes from his state of flatness, which seemed indecent, unnatural. I couldn't believe that he could open his eyes and speak, but he did.

"Take my watch," he said.

"You'll be all right," I lied. "Let me call the medic." I dug out my canteen and tried to pour some water into his mouth.

"Nyet," he choked out, "take my watch."

I sat down beside him and took his hand.

"Please," he rasped, blood coming out of his nose and mouth.

I took the watch and held it in my other hand, because it seemed important to him, and I could give him that small thing. The tension left his face, his breathing stopped, and he was gone.

You've seen animals die, on the *kolkhoz*, Yulia. How strange to watch life leave a body, and witness what's left behind. A shell, absolutely still, that used to house a living creature, but now doesn't even look like that creature. Someone had loved this captain, I was sure of it, and he loved them back. But I was the one person to watch him die. Where did the captain go? Was this shell all that was left of him?

I wandered around, stumbling on shards of metal, and realized I was crying. Big, fat tears that came hard and fast. So much devastation, Yulia. We won this battle, but at such a price! And now what? Where to? I turned in a circle, but each direction seemed pointless, one path no better than another.

I spotted Solomatin, slumped over on a fallen tree, head in hands, and made my way toward him, dodging metal and gore.

I collapsed onto the log next to him. "What a day," I said, still sniffling.

"A banner day for Death," he said after a minute. "She is everywhere. Do you feel her?"

I took in the scene from where we sat, alert for Baba Yaga, half expecting her to come charging out of the charred woods, but saw only the same bodies, the same fires, the same smoking piles of metal. But I felt her there, in the destruction. Baba Yaga was there, wearing her Death mask, taking care not to be seen.

My eyes settled on the dead captain, a small dark stain on the distant ground. I hoped they'd bury him.

Solomatin was low. He'd lost hundreds, maybe a thousand, from his division, some of them good comrades. It was a hard moment, sitting there amongst the destruction, but it occurred to me that these men had died as warriors, for the Motherland, and wasn't that worthy, even glorious? But when I said as much to Solomatin he gave me a dark look, then shrugged. "*Da*, I suppose, but what does that matter to them? They've been erased."

La! So strange. I didn't know this man well, didn't want to argue with a senior commander for the glory of his troops' sacrifices, but I thought he was missing something in his grief. Death doesn't erase the things people do in their lives, the things they accomplish. That captain helped take down a German tank, and was probably the one who gave the order. All those dead soldiers helped us to win this battle, and that's important. Things like that have consequences that live on.

I went back to camp with Solomatin, where everyone was busy counting troops, sorting out who was still alive. I had no one to count, since I'd gone rogue from my platoon, so I wandered around until I realized I was starving, and wolfed down two bowls of soup at the field kitchen, with half a loaf of bread. There was no rationing, as they'd lost more than half their men in the battle. But maybe some were taken to the field hospital.

Suddenly, I'm exhausted. Seems years since I've slept through a whole night. I'm going to curl up near the fire, under my *plash palatka*. Good night, my Yulia.

14.7.44

Sergei's letters are *gone*, Yulia! They were in my pack before he left, but they're not there now. God and Hell, Misha, what have you done? If you're still alive at the end of this, I'll kill you.

But what if it wasn't Misha? What if someone else found the packet and gave it to a bluecap, or worse, to Shapiro, or some other commissar? No, must have been Misha. I'd be in prison, or dead, if the Party knew.

Must have searched through my things while I slept, and like a common thief, stolen the one thing I wouldn't have given him freely. Maybe he took it out of concern for me, even love, but if he really cared, wouldn't he respect my wishes? Wouldn't that be a stronger proof of affection? Gah. My head hurts.

16.7.1944

I'm stuck in Nikolai Solomatin's camp, surrounded by Germans, waiting for reinforcements. Solomatin has barely left my side these past two days, and has been doing his best to be handsome and interesting with me. His words are too pretty to be trusted, but I like that he doesn't try to protect me. That he tries to kiss me, says he loves me, *I don't* like. He loves me—seriously? I don't believe it and I don't love him. I love Misha. I really do, even though I'm mad at him. But I'm terrified for him, Yulia! I actually said a prayer for him, tried to make a deal with God to let him be all right, and I don't even believe in God. I wonder if that would influence his listening.

It's true I'll do anything, if only Misha comes back on his own feet. That he should die for Sergei, who has killed so many, who found his conscience only when his Maria was threatened. That he should die to protect me. I couldn't bear it.

I do like Solomatin, as a friend. I wouldn't want to see him die either. Yesterday, we ran together along the Nemen, to scout the Fritz situation, under a brilliant sun that sent sparks off the river. We came to a very high bank and I had some trouble getting up the steep side, so Nikolai gave me his hand and pulled me up, and tried to kiss me. *Stoy*, I said, and I laughed, not because I liked it, but because I was so alive in that moment, looking out from the top of the hill, everything sharp and beautiful, extra real and not real at the same time. Remember those French paintings Aunt Agnes took us to see? Paul Somebody. Cezanne. Paul Cezanne. It was like being inside one of his paintings. Then came machine gun fire and we dropped back down into the bushes by the water, and continued to run. When night came, it came fast and black, and we could move more freely in its shadow. Found a village full of Germans, important to avoid, so we skirted around and came to a farmstead on a hill, where we climbed into an old hay cart to sleep. There, Nikolai sang to me, softly, because of the Germans, or maybe that was an excuse—*Dark eyes, passionate eyes, burning and beautiful eyes, how I love you, how I fear you, seems we met in an unfortunate hour…*

Back at camp now, still alive. Nikolai is too smooth, too persistent, and I want to get out of here. Let's hope the reinforcements have wings on their feet.

**11 July 1944
Bereznik**

*Senior Sergeant Roza Shanina
184th Rifle Division, Fifth Army
Third Belorussian Front*
Dear Roza,

The deed is done, and I hope you will forgive me for deceiving you. I've seen your father and found him astonishingly normal, with just one head and no scales on his body at all. He was civil, almost cordial, although I'm not sure that he appreciated the gift I brought for him.

I'm at the train station now, awaiting transport to 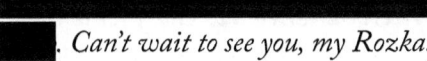. *Can't wait to see you, my Rozka.*

*Love—
Misha*

16.7.44
Rear camp at Vilnius

Thank the gods, Yulia! Misha survived delivering that cursed letter. My anger for him has gone, has slipped off entirely like the green headscarf I lost yesterday. What a Misha! He solved my problem and helped my family, and came to no harm. How did I get so lucky to find such a boyfriend? I wonder what you thought of him when he came to Yedma. You must have noticed how handsome he is, how well he speaks. I wonder if you can see us together, after this war. If you would like to have such a brother-in-law.

18.7.44

We worked the *Katyushnik* trench again today, and received a delivery at midday with a tin of *shchi*,[37] bread, and letters. I'd missed breakfast so was reaching for the bread when the runner handed me a letter, and I saw the small, thin scrawl of the writer. Papa! Misha had delivered Sergei's letter to him—this must be in response to that. Holding my breath, I opened it and read—

> *Dear Roza,*
>
> *I was surprised to see your face in the Moscow paper, and to learn that you've received a Medal of Glory for combat actions. Perhaps the discipline of being a soldier in the Red Army has cured you of your headstrong selfishness. I'm glad for it.*

---

37   *Shchi*—a Russian cabbage soup.

I write today about your eldest brother and the shame he has brought upon our family. Do nothing for him. He must learn what happens to those who defy orders, and we must detach ourselves from him if we are to stay in ▇ *good graces. I'm confident that you, my daughter, would not aid a traitor to the Party. It would end my career, and possibly my life.*

Your father,
Yegor Shanin

I read it through twice before I fully understood—Papa would not help. Yegor the Lame will lean on his crutch and kiss Stalin's hand, while his favorite son starves in prison.

"*Mudak!*" I swore, and tore the paper in half.

"Is it Misha?" Sasha asked, looking alarmed.

Sasha had jumped up at my outburst and Kali looked up from where she leaned against the trench wall, reading her own letter. They both looked worried, even scared. I shook my head, about to say that I was sorry I couldn't tell them, when I realized, maybe I could. Why not? The deed was done. The reason to hide it no longer existed.

"Not Misha, it's my loving father," I said, crumpling the letter into a ball.

"Your father! Your *dead* father?" Kali asked sharply.

I looked at her in surprise. Had I told them that Papa was dead? I do that sometimes. It's just easier. But Sasha and Kali deserved to know the truth.

"He's not dead, but he should be," I said, very angrily.

They looked at each other and then at me, in a considering sort of way that I wasn't sure I liked, waiting for me to continue. But I wasn't going to go through the whole sordid history of my relationship with my father in that moment.

"This is about my brother Sergei," I said, and went on to tell them the whole story, including the contents of both letters, the argument with Misha, and his stealing the letters and delivering them to Papa in Yedma. I thought it would be difficult to say out loud, but the words just spilled out of me, running over each other in my eagerness.

They were a great audience! I had their total attention and sympathy throughout the telling, and when I got to part about Beria's sound-proof office and his appetite for young girls, Sasha clapped her hands over her mouth and Kali got real agitated, saying "and this, the head of our secret police!"

Afterward, I felt lighter than I had in ages. Such a relief to have it out in the open, and to see their reactions, which made me feel good because they mirrored my own.

Sasha grasped me in a hug, and this time I met the embrace gratefully.

"Oh Roza, you've been carrying this with you for months and didn't say anything?"

I cried a little then, feeling huge affection for my friends. It didn't take long to convince them that I hadn't wanted them to be involved in any way.

"I'm afraid to ask, but what does your father write?" this from Kali.

"Yegor Shanin won't help." I laughed bitterly, and held the letter out to Kali, still crushed in my fist.

Kali smoothed out the crumpled halves of paper and she and Sasha read together. I didn't watch them but turned away, feeling terrible again, ashamed of my family. Now they knew where I came from — that my brother was a blue cap, that Papa is an old Bolshevik. I wasn't worried that they would think less of me, I just didn't like them knowing.

"My goodness," I heard Sasha say. I looked up to meet her blue eyes, crinkled with concern. She seemed to be searching for something to rally around, and finally said—"Maybe this is just his first reaction."

Kali murmured in agreement. "That could be," she said, nodding at Sasha. "It's shocking news, hard for any parent. Maybe he'll come around after he's had some time."

"Yes, that's what I'm thinking," Sasha said, in a relieved sort of way. "He is Sergei's father. And you say Sergei was his favorite, right? He'll come around to help."

I heard the words but shook my head. Papa wouldn't do anything to put himself in danger, this I knew. But I felt a tiny seed of hope, in spite of myself. Could my friends be right?

20.7.44

Day off today and lots of mail, including some letters from total strangers, which has been happening more often since that article came out in the Canadian paper. "Unseen Terror of Eastern Prussia" they called me, with a stock photo of me and my rifle. Ha! Most of the letters are from soldiers who ask for a picture or a few words. I feel strange about it, embarrassed, I guess. I don't know what to say to these guys so I don't respond.

Also, a letter from Solomatin. My first thought was to burn it—I'm still so angry with him. But I was weak, and ripped it open, curious to see what he had written.

He loves me. He misses me. In the whole world there is no one he wants so much as he wants me, and he's sorry that he upset me, that I ran away.

I must have blushed, or reacted in an obvious way, because Sasha and Kali were suddenly looking at me and wanting to know who the letter was from.

"Nicolai Solomatin," I said. "Listen to this—'Noble Falcon, wherever you go, my heart will be with you—'"

"So romantic," Sasha sighed, and complained about Toska never writing her, and then—"But what about Misha? I thought you were back with him."

Kali didn't give me a chance to answer, so eager was she to know if this was the same captain I'd been trapped with last week, and the same Nikolai Solomatin who used to hang around with the *Katyushniks*. When I said that it was, she got visibly upset. Apparently she and Duce had an encounter with him at the inn, and Duce told her that not only is he married, but he has a mistress in every town between Vitebsk and Vilnius!

"God and Hell!" I exclaimed. There must be some mistake! Could there be two guys called Nikolai Solomatin? I described him carefully, and yes, it seemed Kali and I had met the same Nikolai.

"Did he force himself on you?" Kali asked, leaning forward, her voice tight in that way she gets when she's on the lookout for men behaving badly toward women. I assured her that he did not, that nothing had happened, really, although he had certainly tried.

But Nikolai Solomatin, a skirt chaser! I knew I couldn't trust him, and I should have burned the letter without reading it. I'm so disappointed in him, and more, Yulia. He betrayed me. We shared an adventure, a connection, that had felt real. He wrote in his letter that he loved me, and only me. Lies, all lies! Men are horrible, Yulia. I can't think why we want to be like them.

But it could have been much worse. I've heard a lot of stories. Masha, in my own platoon, had a terrible experience as a kept "army wife" for Colonel K—a slave to that man's desires.

I scanned the letter one last time for signs of treachery. *Beautiful Roza, with eyes of fire and ice.*

"Pretty little lies," I said, "written in smoke, while Misha is fire, and the wood that feeds it."

Sasha advised that I never talk to Solomatin again, and never explain myself, and that seemed like a good plan. Misha is my love. I wanted to burn the letter straight away, but it was the middle of the day in our billet (day off and all) so there was no fire. I'll do it tonight, in one of the many fires that always spring up after dark.

20.7.44

Oh Yulia, how I wish I had burned that letter from Solomatin right away and not forgotten about it. Misha got back this afternoon and went to our billet, but instead of finding me, he found Solomatin's letter, lying on my bunk where I left it. God and Hell, he is so angry with me, and I feel two inches tall. This man risked his life to help me, and now what is he thinking?

I tried to talk to him at supper, but he was so stiff, his face a rocky place, and when I tried to thank him, he pulled a wad of paper out of his pocket and threw it at me. Solomatin's letter.

"Nothing happened, Misha. I swear on my life that nothing happened."

"On your life? Nothing you care about, then," he said, in a stone-cold voice, and walked away.

I was eager to defend myself, eager to tell him about Papa's letter, but I didn't chase after him. Because what did I do that was so bad? I fended Solomatin off, and ran away from him! How can I help it if he wants me and writes me letters? If only Misha would listen, he would understand how it is for us girls, how I did the best I could. How much my heart belongs to him.

2.8.44

I stayed in the rear these past two weeks, trying to be a good commander, a good soldier who does as she's told. I don't think I've ever been so sad and tired, and it doesn't help that I have my monthly. Been moving around in a fog, like a lifeless puppet, "on watch" for dangers that don't exist, with Misha giving me the silent treatment. He's unreasonable. What did I do that was so wrong?

And Papa, refusing to help Sergei. These men are going to kill me, Yulia! I've put off writing to Sergei, but he needs to know what Papa wrote. But what can I say? "Sorry our father is such a *mudak*. Hope you find a way out on your own." I don't want to write that letter, don't want to be the messenger of doom for my oldest brother.

I cried into my vodka while the rest of the army liberated Trakai, and came to a decision. I would go where the battles are taking place. There was nothing holding me in the rear. But which battles, which Front? Important to avoid Solomatin, to the north, so I thought of Horopov, to the southeast.

I got a note from Malchonov yesterday, saying he'll be here tomorrow, passing through on his way south. I wonder if he would give me a lift? Either way, I need to write that letter to Sergei if I'm going to see Malchonov. I'll be as kind as possible and put out Sasha's idea that Papa might change his mind, but I don't really believe it, and I don't think Sergei will either.

6.8.44

Dear Yulia,

It's been a busy few days since I've written anything in my journal. I caught a lift south with Pyotr, hiding in the back of his Willys in my camouflage until he gave the "all clear." Then I got to sit up and watch Lithuania fly past, the wind in my hair, sun on my face. I love traveling by jeep. It's like going by horse cart, only on a comfortable seat, and moving ten times as fast.

Pyotr dropped me off at Horopov's headquarters, and with a quick "*spasibo*,[38] comrade," I jumped out and went straight inside to report for duty. Trouble was, Horopov wasn't there, and Shapiro, Blokhin's commissar, was almost the first person I saw.

"What are you doing here?" He asked, almost yelling.

Damn! How was it possible? We weren't even close to our home division!

My mind rattled about for an answer, but no luck. "Reporting for duty, comrade Commissar," I mumbled.

He snorted and asked for my orders. I fished around in my pockets for a minute and tried to appear surprised at not finding them.

Shapiro pushed a finger into my face. "Back to the rear!"

I had an impulse to bite that finger, a mere two inches from my teeth, but I resisted. Shapiro might be a little *podkhalim*,[39] but I wasn't a savage.

"How will I get back?" I asked. Last time he had dumped me into a field and let me fend for myself, but now I was a very long way from my unit, couldn't just skip home.

Shapiro looked at me like I was some kind of slug and told me to catch a ride in any of the supply trucks that are constantly moving between camps. I ground my teeth and nodded, thankful that at least he wasn't going to escort me onto one of the trucks.

Outside, I walked around camp looking for the supply depot, found it easily and was on the brink of asking for a lift home, when a band of *Katyushas* motored past, toward the border. I watched them for a minute, and noticed lots of other units moving out, and

---

38 *Spasibo*—Russian for "thank you."

39 *Podkhalim*—Russian for "boot licker" or "toady."

everyone else looked like they were getting ready. These troops were pushing the line forward, Yulia! My whole body ached with desire to go with them. And why shouldn't I? I don't take orders from Shapiro, and here was an opportunity to be useful to my people, and to be engaged with life instead of rotting in the rear.

I wasn't where I was supposed to be, and I'd been told to go back. But how would I ever become a fierce and extraordinary warrior by taking the easy way, the safe way out? The rear isn't the place for me — that truth is clear. I need action. It's not as if I'm fighting for my own life, I'm fighting for my people, for my country. I'm not afraid to die for the happiness of others, so why did I feel guilty, turning away from that supply depot, when my actions would forward the common good?

Conflicted, determined, I headed toward the artillery guys, like a horse to its barn. The very first unit I came upon was excited to see me, they'd seen my picture in the paper. "Come with us!" they said, and so I did. Fun, cheerful guys, always on the move, singing, throwing out jokes, basically respectful. No one tried to grab me, and I was grateful. We marched for three days, marches that took up every hour of sunlight, long treks across fields of rye and crabgrass, through forests of half-hanging trees, across quick rivers that sparkled in the sun. No battles, but I was content to be at the very front of formations, always moving, pushing the frontline further into Lithuania. I was almost cheerful. Who cares about Misha or Papa or Sergei, if I could live like this, on the frontlines?

We marched twenty kilometers yesterday, and had just stopped for the night when I got an angry note from Blokhin. I don't know how the devil he keeps finding me, Yulia. I wanted to run and hide so I wouldn't be forced to the rear, but my body was dead weight from all the marching, and the boys were so good — it was hard to leave. They fell asleep, and so did I.

A kick woke me up.

"Orders are orders, go to the rear," said Blokhin's toadie. It wasn't Shapiro, but he didn't seem any better. He *kicks* me awake?

Two machine gunners had been stirred from their sleep by the commotion, and watched with pity as I gathered my things and left with the little man. He took me in a Willys all the way back to headquarters at Obukhovo, where Blokhin was waiting, like a giant spider.

Blokhin looked down his nose at me, very stern.

"Sergeant Shanina, you have ignored direct orders and put yourself in danger. What do you have to say for yourself?"

"I was marching with the artillery guys," I said.

"On whose orders?" he roared.

I tried to think of something good to say, but he spared me the effort by continuing on.

"Why are you so careless with your life? You must have known you were within meters of the *shtrafbat*. As your commanding officer, and as a friend who wants to see you stay alive, I insist that you return to your unit before you get killed or charged with a military crime."

As a friend? I thought, but said—"It's not a crime to go to the Front."

"Without orders? It's against the rules, Shanina. Don't get too comfortable."

I felt a thrill of fear as he delivered those words, under his breath, right in my face. He was right, I knew he was right. With enough power, anything can be a crime. Just look at Sergei's situation! I had no argument to make, but I did have a question.

"Comrade Captain, why look for me? It seems you pay more attention to where I go, what I do, than you do the other girls."

"The other girls don't go where they're not supposed to," he said, but his eyes were shifty. We both knew that wasn't exactly true.

"And, I've been ordered to keep you safe," he said after harumphing around and clearing his throat a few times.

This was very strange, Yulia. And confusing. "Ordered by who?"

"Someone who likes to see your face in the papers."

"But who—"

"Don't push me," Blohkin snarled, and I forced my mouth shut and directed my eyes to the center of his chest, like a good soldier.

He told me to go back to my platoon on the spot, and threatened to charge me with "dereliction of duty" and "failure to carry out orders" if he caught me at the Front again without orders.

I left, sullenly. Pavel Blohkin, bah! Ordering me around like a wayward cow. He is my senior commander, but still. And what the devil was going on with this order to keep me safe? Who would have issued such an order, and what did it mean?

Someone who likes to see your face in the papers.

I took my time getting back to the rear, stopped by supply to pick up some rations and a new camouflage, and when I got to the place we'd been camped—no platoon! Only a faint memory of our tent. I had no idea where they'd gone or what I should do, so I flagged down a passing ZIS and caught a lift to headquarters.

The truck was full of communications guys. I've always gotten along with the comm guys, and if I wasn't a sniper, I might like to do that type of work. It seems really interesting, like you'd have to use your brain and think strategically. Sergei was head of a comm unit, before he got arrested. Although I don't think he did the traditional job of laying wire and so on, I suspect it was more like spying on German communications. That sort of thing.

In the end, I was able to hunt down my platoon, found the tent Sasha and Kali had set up and I'm settled back in with them. It was late when I got here, after curfew, and they were sound asleep. I dreaded having to deal with one-and-a-half-Ivans, but he's disappeared, and no one has any idea what happened to him! Gone, like a memory. The new guard, Alexei, is not so surly, and he watched me crawl into camp without comment.

It was good to get away for a while, although I didn't see any combat. Was it worth it? I don't know, Yulia. I don't know why I keep leaving, and I don't know why Blokhin has orders to keep me safe. I guess I don't know much of anything these days, except that I'm sad, and I don't know the reason for that either. Misha, or Sergei, or war—I guess it's all lying heavily with me just now. And the "orders to keep me safe" makes me ill. I don't want the platoon to find out, because it seems like special treatment, just the sort of thing some of the girls would resent and hate me for. But not Sasha and Kali, who love me even if they don't always understand me. Thank the gods for our *troika*.

7.8.44
Rear camp near Vilnius

Found out today from Sasha that Misha was sent out while I was gone, along with Toska and a slew of artillery guys. They probably went northeast, since that's our path forward, and I wonder if he will run into Nikolai Solomatin's battalion. What would they say to each other? Would they fight?

Don't borrow trouble, Mama whispers in my mind's ear, and I agree. Nothing good comes from brooding.

I've reconciled myself with staying in the rear camp with my platoon. With Blokhin stalking me, it won't be possible to sneak away. Do you think Papa gave Blokhin that order? I'm not sure he has the power, as a local Party Director, and frankly I'm not sure he cares if I live or die. You won't like me saying that, but really, he did kick me out into the streets when I was fourteen. If Fyodor hadn't taken me in, I'd probably be dead, at Papa's hands.

I'm afraid someone in the Party gave the order, that they want to turn me into another "Lady Death." I should have trusted my first instinct—I should never have let Malchonov publish that first article! And now it's too late to back out, because I've given three other interviews with photo shoots, and at least one of those has been published because Solomatin's guard saw it, and a guy in the communications truck too. People are starting to recognize me wherever I go, and now this order to keep me safe.

It's true I've earned two Medals of Glory, one with orders and one on a rogue mission, but why do I deserve fame? Most of my days are spent lying around the rear camp, while others fight and die every day and no one sees them. Probably half my kills occurred in battles that I was not supposed to be fighting. The papers glorify my bravery, while Blokhin yells at me. I believe I am brave, when it comes to combat, and I've never been good at obeying, but which of these is better, which is truly worthy of glory? God, I hope it's bravery, although I intend to be as obedient as a little lamb for as long as I can stand it.

If the Party wants to turn me into Propaganda Girl—The Girl with the Golden Rifle, or something—and if they intend to keep me out of danger and tell lies about what I'm doing, I'm not having it. If they want me to be brave and take part in real battles, that would be all right. I would go along with that. That might even be good. It would be worth it to have my picture spread around if it keeps me on the frontlines.

7.8.44, 22:10
New billet in Vilnius, Stray Troika quarters

Vilnius has fallen, and everyone is in a grand mood! The whole Front moved today, and it was once again so thrilling to see everyone move together, to be part of it, to feel the tremendous power of our gigantic army and its machinery taking back our land from the Nazis. When we arrived at Vilnius, we found that we're billeted to a house once more, and none of us objected. It's a thin building, but has four walls and a ceiling, and we won't be here long, now that the *fashisty*[40] are on the retreat.

Celebrations were underway when we arrived, and there was plenty of vodka, plenty of music. Sasha, Kali and I went by the artillery guys for some fun, but I got distracted when I saw Toska, because Misha's not back and no one has news of him. If Toska's back, why isn't Misha?

When I got home tonight, just a little while ago, I poured out everything to Misha in a letter, told him that I've never been more certain that I love him, and only him. But there's nowhere to send it. I've been thinking about going after him, tracking him down, but I'm trying to be good. I know the general area where he might be, and Toska tells me it's very hot, under constant fire, which makes me imagine the worst.

Where are you honey, where, where are you, where are you, wherever the war took you...

Misha is smart, very capable. He even got Sergei's letter to Yedma. He's not dead, just something else has happened, right? But he *could* be, Yulia! One bomb, in just the right place, and it wouldn't matter how good, smart, capable or anything. And what would I do, if he's been killed? Find a way to carry on. God and Hell.

---

40 *Fashisty*—a Russian term meaning "fascist" that was considered extremely offensive during WWII.

12.8.44

Left yesterday morning in a mushroom rain, grateful for good boots, determined to find Misha, or someone who knows what happened to him. It's been two weeks since Toska got back—Misha should be home. The *Katyushniks* never missed me, I'm not sure they even knew I was gone. Such is the importance of our current duties, Yulia. Caught a ride in a ZIS to headquarters at Gorodok, and asked there if anyone had news of Sergeant Mikhail Panarin, but no luck. Only one gunner said there were still some artillery units near no-man's land, or what had been no-man's land before lines were redrawn. The wave of hope drowned in my stomach when I realized it was strange these guys didn't know Misha. There weren't so many troops here, don't they all eat from the same kitchen? Wouldn't they know Misha? Unless he was killed early on.

But I wouldn't give up. I'd come this far, I would see it through to the end, no matter how hard.

The light rain had turned vicious and churned the road into a swamp—the mud kept swirling up and trying to grab the boots off my feet. I stomped on, maybe ten kilometers, my *plash palatka* wrapped around me so entirely that I had just a small opening for my face. *Like a beast of burden, wearing blinders*, I thought. My progress was slow, unsatisfying. Step-yank, step-yank, all the time thinking of Misha, praying to a God I don't believe in that he was alive, that he still loved me. Each step added another stone to my stomach. He was dead, I knew he was dead. I wanted to stop walking, turn around, keep the blinders on.

Voices came through the falling water, Russian voices, and I pulled the plastic off my head to have a look around, but no Misha, just a group of scouts. I asked if they'd seen any light tanks around.

"There's one stuck in a ditch a couple of kilometers down the road," came the answer, and I looked toward the horizon, desperate to see Ferdinand, but saw only a wall of water, pouring from the sky with determination.

The path was very bad now, a river of mud, and I had to look at my feet to stay on them. But I had new energy, spawned from hope, and I step-yanked with purpose, looking out for Ferdinand and my Misha. Came round a corner and saw the nose of a big gun sticking out of a ravine, and running as best as I could, I came to the edge of the ditch and saw two guys up to their knees in water, pushing the gun from behind.

Misha! Their backs were to me, but I knew it was him, from the way he held his shoulders, the bend to his back. *Still alive!* I wanted to shout, to whoop out my relief, but I stayed quiet, not wanting to cause a distraction that might send the gun back on top of them. I stood there, on the edge of the ditch, tensed and wanting to jump in to help, unsure if I would be welcome.

Ten minutes later, the gun went over the top, and Misha paused to rest, hands on his knees.

"Good show," I called, clapping.

His head turned toward me, and then he lurched up and faced me directly. "Roza!"

"Misha!" I cried, laughing.

He powered himself out of the ravine and stopped just in front of me. "You came to find me?"

I threw my arms around him and hung on tight. "*Da*, naturally," I said, breathing him in. He hugged me back, hard, and I couldn't help adding some tears to the rain on my face. He still loved me.

We rode Ferdinand back to the scouts, where it was Misha's turn to be night guard. I stayed with him, keeping watch in the rain. It turned very cold, with me wearing just panties and bra beneath my camouflage, and when our watch ended and we were free to go, I was frozen, shaking with cold. Misha fetched me a fresh *telnyashka* and a new camouflage suit from the supply truck but my fingers could not work the buttons and strings, so he dressed me, like a brother, with hands that were somehow warm, and then he wrapped himself around me to give me his warmth. Did not even try to kiss me, or talk to me, he just took care of me, and the flame in my heart grew stronger, so grateful to have my Misha back. Next morning, this morning, I left him with a real smile in my heart, knowing he would come back to me when he could. We hadn't even talked about our fight, but it doesn't matter anymore.

15.8.44

Not much action in the *Katyushnik* trench today, so we passed the time tallying up our kills. My count was highest—36 dead little Hitlers. Sasha was next with 25, then Lida with 22 and Kaleriya with 18. Naturally my kill count is higher, because I've run away to the Front and had more opportunity to shoot, but some of the girls didn't like it. *That's not a true count*, Nastya sneered. To be honest, my count is probably higher than what I've written down, but I didn't argue. Didn't want to defend myself on this of all things. She's just jealous, or maybe she's angry that I don't stay back with them. Maybe she feels abandoned by her commander. But I've been with the platoon for two whole weeks, Yulia, except for the one day I went after Misha. And what's so wrong with going to the Front? I don't think it's so wrong to leave the girls, with them having such easy orders.

It's just the way things have gone, really. If I could make a change, change the Red Army's policy against women at the Front, or change myself to be less compulsive, less driven, I'd do it in a second.

But these things are set on their path, like a great, rushing river that gallops over everything. I can't fight against it.

20.8.44
Ferdinand's cab, near Poland

We're on the move constantly now, pushing the *fashisty* back through Lithuania. Left our billet in Vilnius after just one week, and marched for two days, and now we've stopped, near the southwestern border of Lithuania, where the Shirvanta flows into the Sesupe. It's dank and musty here, I'm told it's always like this, good farmland, perfect for growing crops, but like everywhere along the war arena, the green has been stomped out and I doubt anything has grown here in years. We pitched our tent near the river, and lovely as it is to hear the rushing water, it's also unnerving. Would we even hear an attack? But we won't be here long. Sasha stays with Toska at night, and I with Misha. A lot of the girls go by their boyfriends.

I am now in Ferdinand's cab, which is warm and dry, waiting for Misha to come home from the men's rally. It's still early, but it's been a long day and I don't know how much longer I'll be able to stay awake. I want to write while I have the chance.

This afternoon I was pulled out of the trench to meet a man who arrived in an airplane with orders to fly me somewhere tomorrow morning for a photo shoot. Yashka Gudkov, he was called. Very strange-looking, with dark pencil painted around his eyes and the ends of his mustache greased into curls, like a ringmaster from the Moscow Circus, and he had a snobbish air, like he was doing me a favor to speak with me. He struck me as someone I could not like.

Gudkov told me he had news of Sergei, and wanted to take me to dinner. I had to accept, had to hear his news, whether I wanted to or not. But the dinner was good, with fresh milk, and after a lot of hints and questions, he told me in a pointy, flowery voice that Sergei was in a Moscow prison, sentenced to ten years hard labor. He didn't know any more than I did, Yulia, and I was sorry to have suffered his company to no advantage.

"What! Has he been sent to Siberia?" I asked, hoping my voice didn't sound wooden, that Gudkov wouldn't suspect that I already knew all of this.

"He's now in a Moscow prison," came the answer, "awaiting another trial."

Gudkov pasted on a sympathetic face and droned on about "dereliction of duty" and "abuse of power," but there were smug lines around his mouth. I've seen this kind of man before—a man who feeds his own importance with other men's failures. Loathsome, Yulia. I left shortly after, thanked him for dinner and hurried off, not caring what he thought. I ran straight to Ferdinand, and here I sit, bundled up in our woolen blanket, waiting for my love.

Ah, Sergei! Always the favorite, the first-born child, a son. The boy who turned everything he touched to gold. I know he was kind to you, Yulia, but Sergei always made me feel small—I was beneath his notice. Papa doted on him, his little soldier, and he spat at me, his lazy cow. But now, at the moment when Sergei really needs his help, Papa refuses. I guess Sergei's become as inconvenient to Papa as I have always been.

I feel terrible for Sergei. I may have resented him when we were growing up in Ukraine, but being the Golden Boy didn't stop him from doing those horrible things. He must have thought he was doing right, doing his duty, supporting his country, suppressing his doubts, and now he's as good as dead. How could he have known it would turn out so badly? Could I have gone down the same path, in the name of vengeance?

Dig a hole for someone, and you will fall into it, Mama says, and that seems right. Sergei has dug a lot of holes.

And I, I have killed a lot of Germans. Sasha insists we aren't killing people, that we are killing fascists, and that doesn't count, but can it be true? Fedya and Mikhail were killed by the Nazis, who think us "sub-human." Seems like a trick, that we each think the other side aren't real people.

How can we know that we're doing the right thing, when everything is smoke and mirrors? I know nothing, Yulia, except that Truth is hard to find. But I do know what's real to me, and maybe Kali was right, that what we see and think is true has more power over us than an objective truth that we can't find. I know that I love you, Yulia, and Misha, and Sasha and Kali, and that I belong in combat. These are the things that hold power over me. But they're written on water, because my life is written on water. When I die, does my truth disappear, does the love I feel end?

God, so serious. Everyone will die, that's a real truth, an *istina* truth that can't be changed, so why think about it? I don't, really, but it feels close now, like Baba Yaga is lurking in the woods, watching for her chance to grab me. It's all of this thinking about our brothers that's done it. I need to shake this mood.

Fell asleep holding my pencil, and still no Misha. Where can he be? But Fedya came to me while I slept. He was in the cab with me, although I couldn't see him, rather I knew it was him that surrounded me, like a warm sunset. He wrapped his whole self around me, and I felt totally safe, with no fear, no needs grasping at me.

"Shhhh," he whispered. "Everything is as it should be. You are good enough, you are strong enough."

A feeling of peace spread over me, like all of the earth's sadness and joy had come together to swirl around me, gently, singling me out to give me peace. I've never been so comforted, Yulia, and I was so grateful, in my dream, for sweet Fedya. I turned to thank him, to hug him, but he was gone, and I woke up.

But somehow, he's still here, my big brother watching over me. He'll be with me tomorrow, when I go on that blasted photo shoot with Gudkov in his airplane, and while I listen to him drone on about Sergei's mistakes. I'll have Fedya with me, and Misha will be home soon. And there's something else, Yulia, something I've just realized. I still feel Fedya's love, and I've felt it all along. His love didn't stop, so maybe mine won't either.

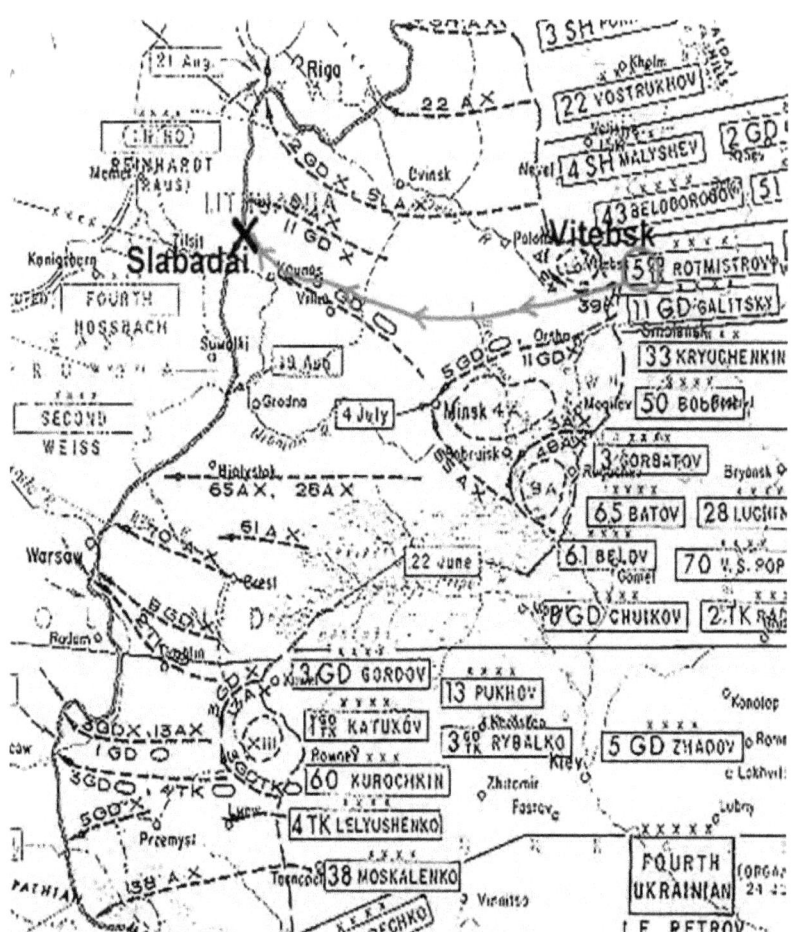

The 5th Army's route from Vitebsk to Slabadai in late summer, 1944. The line along the western side marks the border with German-occupied territory.

THIRD JOURNAL:
AUTUMN

30.8.44
Platoon tent

Misha got the Medal of Courage last night, at assembly, for "exemplary bravery and valor while surrounded by enemy forces near Vitebsk." So proud of him, and only a little jealous. But I don't think it meant much to him, Yulia. He looked at it closely, then gave it to me. I thought to pin it on him, but he shook his head.

"These things always sound better than they actually were," he said.

"You earned it," I said, but he just shrugged.

"You keep it, and send it to my mother if I'm killed."

That sobered me up, and I dropped the subject. I'll be receiving my second Order of Glory soon, and to be honest I'm looking forward to it. But everyone has different feelings, so I took his medal, wrapped it up with mine in my blue scarf and put it in my rucksack, where I hope it will stay until the end of the war.

The *Katyushniks* are fun guys, good friends, and seem to be always ready for a party. Tonight, they planned to celebrate all the medals that were handed out, and Misha and I were happy to join in. We had just headed out in their direction when I spied Blokhin at a short distance, coming toward us down the path that has been trampled into the ground behind the line of guns. I dove behind the closest gun to hide. I acted on instinct, because we weren't doing anything wrong. I just didn't want to face Blokhin.

I spotted Misha from my hiding place, peering around the gun's rear end and looking at me like I was crazy. He started toward me but I waved him off vigorously, gesturing in Blokhin's direction.

And then Blokhin was upon us, and I heard him talking to Misha, asking him where I was. I knew it! Trying to hunt me down again. But how the devil does Blokhin know to ask Misha about me? I'm sure he doesn't know that Sasha is with Toska, for example. I think he's been having me followed, Yulia. It's the only way he could know so much about where I go and what I do.

Just then, Blokhin was saying that some generals had arrived at camp and wanted to meet me, having seen a couple of newspaper articles, and blah blah blah. I was glad to be hidden. I'd much rather go by the *Katyushniks* than get roped into entertaining some stodgy generals. But that wasn't all Blokhin wanted, he also asked Misha for his help in keeping me away from the frontlines and "out of danger."

"Comrade Stalin likes to see her face in the papers, thinks it's good for morale," he said. "Puts a good face on the People's Army."

Blood rushed to my ears and my lungs stopped working. *Stalin!* My legs threatened to stop working as well, so I sat on the ground and put my head in my hands. Was it possible that *Stalin* was the one who wanted me safe? Did he admire me? Pleasure stabbed through the dread at this thought, which turned to shame, and embarrassment.

"*Da*, comrade Captain," Misha was saying. Much more respectfully than I would have managed.

Soon after, Misha appeared around the side of the gun, his mouth twisted into a crooked smile. "All clear, comrade *Stalina*."

"Don't call me that," I snapped.

Misha sat down heavily with of whoosh of air and grabbed my hand. "Papa Stalin likes the way you look," he said darkly.

I smacked him on the shoulder. "When a lobster whistles on a mountain," I hissed. "It's just what I was afraid of. They must want to use me. The Politburo, I mean."

"Yeah," Misha sighed and gave up trying to make a joke out of it. "I think you're right. A pretty girl sniper who eats fascists for breakfast. Something like that."

We looked at each other and he opened his mouth to say something, and closed it again. A moment later, he gave my fingers a squeeze. "Roza, when this war is over, will you come to Moscow with me?"

What was this? I looked at him and squeezed his hand back. "Changing the subject, I see."

He smiled at me, and he looked so perfect in that moment, with his hair overgrown, oozing sincerity. Young and old and happy and sad all at once.

"*Da*, Misha," I said. "I'd love that."

He leaned against me and touched his head to mine. "I miss Moscow," he said. "We could get a flat on the west side, close to the university, but not too near the Kremlin."

I sighed and closed my eyes against the unbearable pleasure of such an idea. "And have safe, normal lives?"

Misha paused and I watched him stroke his chin, deep in thought. So serious! I had the feeling he was about to go off on a lecture about how safety is an illusion, a crutch for the masses, but he didn't, he just said — "and have safe, normal lives."

I smiled and put my lips to his hand, still clutched in mine. Misha pushed himself up and pulled me next to him, and we headed back toward the rocket boys, walking the two kilometers instead of catching a lift.

It's a new idea that Blokhin would go after Misha to get to me, and I'm not sure what to think. Is he in danger? Am I in danger? I'm desperate to talk to Sasha and Kali about this, especially Kali, and came back to camp after the party for that purpose. But they're not here. No one is, actually. I'm alone. But they'll come back eventually — they've left their rucksacks.

1.9.44

I got a chance to speak with Sasha and Kali this morning, while we were on duty with the *Katyushniks*, scouting for good sniper perches for our new position. The whole platoon was scattered around the woods, so the three of us stood in a tight circle, talking in low voices, while I passed on the incredible news that Stalin had taken a personal interest in me.

"What do think it means?" I asked.

Kali looked serious, with her face screwed up in concentration, but Sasha was obviously impressed. "You'll be *famous*," she said, her eyes big and round, voice full of awe. "With privileges, and special treatment!"

Kali snorted. "How can it be a good thing to have Stalin watching you? Everyone who catches his eye ends up with a bullet in their head!"

"Right, because we're not in danger of that every second of our lives out here," Sasha retorted.

"This is different," Kali insisted, "because Roza would be in danger no matter where she went, and from both sides!"

"I'm not going to be afraid of someone all the way in Moscow. But if he can affect our lives somehow, like maybe get us extra sugar rations—"

I could only laugh at that—Sasha with her sweet tooth. But Kali put her hands on her hips and seemed ready for battle.

"*Stoy*," I said, a bit sharply, "please just help me understand this."

But what was there to be done? We had no way of knowing Stalin's intentions, no way of determining what it all meant.

"They're turning you into a poster child," Kali said, echoing my own fears. I wish I could take it all back! My story, my life.

"I still think the Nazis are the bigger danger," Sasha said, and I'm sure she's right too. We could be killed any day of the week and none of this would matter. Why not take every opportunity for enjoyment that comes along?

They both seemed to think that Misha would be safe, as safe as themselves, in any case, in terms of their relationship with me. God I hope it's true.

Do you remember Pasha? Pavlik Morozov, boy Hero of the Soviet Union, who was killed in the streets by his uncles. You were too young for school when his story was first spread, but it stuck to me hard, and I told you about him. We learned the Pasha song at school, and a dance, and I taught it to you in the kitchen, remember? We'd just gotten to the part where we waved our hands over our heads and sang "pooooor Pasha!" when Papa lost his temper and screamed at us. "Stop that noise or I'll beat you bloody!" and then, while we stood frozen in terror, he said "There is no Pasha, he's a creation, made up to get children to turn their *kulak* parents over to the police." I didn't believe him, and when the statue of Pasha appeared in the plaza in Bereznik, it seemed proof that Papa had lied. But now I realize he was probably speaking the truth. He would have known.

Truth. Right! The ultimate moving target.

22.9.44

The season changed on a breath, and the air is full of rain and sharp down to the bones. My mind's eye sees the trees of Yedma, red and bright gold in a sun that peeps out through the *raputitsa*. Here, the trees are damaged, half-alive. They lost their leaves long before they should have.

New orders came with the new season, and the forward regiment went on attack during the night of the 20th, leaving the rest of us to be "at the ready" to march forward to the new position.

The rains are angry this year, and hurled water at us in a heavy, endless stream while we were tearing down our tents and getting everything ready to go. It was not a friendly time to be packing up to move, and it didn't help that Sasha cried a lot of the time, since she and Toska had split up, but we got everything done, and then huddled in our *plash palatkas* beneath a tree, stamping our boots to keep warm, waiting for the word to march. Misha and Toska and the other artillery guys had gone ahead, paving the way for us to follow. The *Katyushas* had gone even earlier, to inflict as much damage as possible to the enemy before the tanks moved in, than the infantry and artillery. All those brave boys, fighting for all of us, fighting through the downpour, while we dozed on our boots. It was awful, Yulia, bored and trapped as we were, with nothing to do but imagine what was happening. Finally, we got word: Victory! The whole army was to move forward.

Dawn broke as we marched, the rain paused and the sun made a real effort to show itself. I closed my eyes and let its warmth seep into me, and when I opened them again, hundreds of bodies, strewn across the countryside, rain and mud splattered over them such that the earth seemed to be sucking the dead into its belly. *This again*, I thought, and stared at the gray corpses as I marched, looking for Fedya and Mikhail, and now Misha too.

The day trudged on and we eventually reached our assigned quarters—a dugout, a hand-me-down hole in the ground, home for an unknown stretch of time. We'd been marching mostly downhill, coming from the uplands. The land here lays flat and muddy-green, with an occasional mound that seems a sad attempt at a hill. We're still on the western edge of Lithuania, now further north, by the Nemen, which the Lithuanians call "the father of all rivers."

The Nemen is gigantic, Yulia, the biggest river I've ever seen. Maybe it's because Yedma is on the Dvina, but I'm always drawn to rivers. They're always going someplace new, wearing down rocks in its way. Like me. When the rain paused, I went to the Nemen, and stood on the bank for a long time, admiring the stillness of its surface, like a huge slab of glass. I imagined the splash and disturbance if I should hurl myself into the water. She wouldn't care, the Nemen. She would smooth things over quickly.

But then someone called my name, and suddenly there was Misha, coming toward me along the path that had been stamped into the bank.

"Misha!" I ran, and threw my arms around him.

"Oy, *krasotka*,"[41] He said, and staggered back a step, then laughed and put his arms around me. He made to release me after a moment, but I held tight.

"Still alive," I murmured, into his coat front.

"Unless you strangle me to death," he said.

I laughed and relaxed my grip. "This has been the longest day."

"Tell me later," he said, putting his arm around my shoulders and steering me toward camp. "I'm starved!"

Everything is nicer when I know where Misha is, and that he's alive. I worry that I'm becoming too used to him.

7.10.44

Great news today — the army is relaxing their restrictions on the female snipers. *Ypa!* Thank the gods. Now things will get interesting again, and we can do the work we actually signed up to do. Nothing

---

41 *Krasotka* — Russian for "gorgeous."

much else to report, except that we got two new girls this week, and the supply depot finally got new felt boots, which we will take advantage of when the rains end. We are up to fourteen snipers now.

25.10.44

Pyotr Malchonov came for a short visit this morning, but didn't bring a letter from Sergei. It seems he hasn't seen Sergei in a long time, but he's friendly with Sergei's jailor, and that's how he's been getting the letters in and out. Apparently Sergei has been ill, after undergoing an interrogation. I hate to think what that could mean.

The real reason Malchonov came was to tell me about a work opportunity, now that the army had agreed that females can take part in real battles. Captain Aseyev of the 707th is looking for a sniper platoon to support his battalion in Pillkallen, and he's "in a great hurry." I could have kissed Pyotr for thinking of me, although it's not surprising, considering how bitterly I've complained about the "no combat" rule.

"Always in a rush to be shot at," he said dryly.

I stuck my tongue out at him and rushed off to find Degtyarev, who is above Blohkin, to request that my platoon be assigned to Aseyev. I was afraid I'd be ignored, or put off, but he agreed to it right away! Maybe we were the first sniper platoon to ask.

Some of the *devotchkas*[42] did not share my enthusiasm for this assignment. I guess they like sitting around and doing nothing, or else they didn't like how dangerous the mission sounds. It will be dangerous, to be sure. There have been heavy losses on the road to Pillkallen, with the only access from the northeast, which has been

---

42 *Devotchka*—Russian for "girl," with the connotation of virginity.

teeming with landmines and Nazi fortifications until very recently. Not one soldier from the scout party returned, and the next two waves lost most of their troops. We will be part of the fourth wave.

"Why do you always have to be the center of attention?" Nastya Kuzetsova spat out when I briefed the platoon tonight.

I would have laughed at this description of me, so very wrong, if she hadn't looked extremely angry.

"You're going to get us all killed. Maybe you don't care about your own life, but some of us actually want to stay alive," she continued.

And then I got angry, and threatened to write her up for insubordination.

Nastya's face went from red to white, back to red again. "That's fine for you, with all your absences and love affairs!"

God and Hell! Absences and love affairs, and wanting to be the center of attention. How could she have gotten such a wrong idea about my character? Is that what they all thought? Well, the "absences" part wasn't wrong. Maybe I'd left too often, but there was nothing to be done about that now. I needed to make things right with them, needed them to not hate me, or there'd be real trouble getting them to follow my lead.

"We need to look out for each other," I said, thinking out loud. I looked up and saw all of the girls looking back at me.

"I have your backs," I promised. "I will put my life on the line for each and every one of you, and I hope you can say the same. All of you. Because we are going on this mission, and if we don't look out for each other, it'll be a lot more dangerous."

Some of the girls nodded and murmured agreement, but many of them still looked down at their feet.

I pushed on. "We're so close now! Close to pushing these *mudaks* out of our country, these dirty fascists who tried to exterminate us, because they think we're not human, that we don't deserve to be alive!"

I had worked myself into a passion. "Did you come to fight or sit in the rear and eat *kasha*?" I shouted. "Here is our chance! Pillkallen is a key position, and we can help take it!"

"Destroy the enemy!" Lida shouted, and Sasha echoed her, "Destroy the enemy!" and suddenly everyone was shouting and fists were pounding the air, and I was so proud of them, Yulia. My fierce tribe of warriors! We would bring those krauts to their knees at Pillkallen.

Now, as I'm reading this back, I'm not sure that I really sounded like that, talking today. I'm not normally so strong in the way I express myself. But you will know, you will read between the lines, because you know me. And maybe I was that strong, and really did "rally the troops," as they say. This is strange to me—I've always hated telling people what to do, just as I hate someone telling me what to do. And what is "rallying" but an exercise in mind bending, in getting someone to do something they don't want to do? Seems worse than giving a direct order. Because, is it not this "bending" behavior that blurs the real truth? But I didn't lie. I meant what I said.

Everyone can't be right, but I'm commander. Maybe it's every commander's job to boost morale, for the greater good. Papa would say, "the ends justify the means," which he got straight from Stalin, and maybe we all try this on at one time or another. I did something like that today, in motivating my troops, and it didn't feel wrong, Yulia, and I wonder if that should bother me.

I wish Misha was here, but he's gone again for a few days. He'd lighten me up, turn it into a clever joke. Ah, Misha. *V dobry put'*.[43]

---

43   *V dobry put'*—Russian for "good luck."

27.10.44
In a trench, Pillkallen

Yesterday, we boarded a ZIS at 0300 and were transported from Slabadai to Pillkallen. It was a four-hour drive, in total darkness, our headlamps turned off and no moon to guide us. This was intentional—we were moving through heavily fortified German territory and needed to be completely silent and invisible. Twice, I thought we hit a landmine when we bounced roughly over some obstacle or other, but we didn't encounter any real trouble. Degtyarev was right that the clearers did a good job.

The sun was rising as we pulled into camp, and I went in search of the artillery commander, Captain Igor Aseyev, who I knew nothing about except that he was a Hero of the Soviet Union. I found him on a ridge to the west of camp, yelling out orders to his crew as they moved their guns to new positions. He struck me as a great and exceptional warrior. He screamed confidence—power seemed to pour out of his body for several meters in every direction. He greeted me as a true comrade, without any patronization, and I admired him instantly.

Aseyev pointed out the estate we'd been trying to secure, a huge brick house, surrounded by trees and berms, and further out by sheds and smaller buildings. His troops had pushed the Nazis out of the house toward the east two days ago, and he wanted to move in, wanted to use the house as headquarters, but it was too dangerous—the area was still hot with enemy troops.

"How can we best support you?" I asked, wondering if we'd be positioned in the upper windows again, like we'd been at Kozie Gory.

"Trench warfare," he bellowed (everything he said came out as a shout). He told me we'd need to settle in along the berms on the east and south of the manor to keep Fritz from retaking the house, while the big guns would target their camps.

"Why not shoot from the upper level?" I asked, and he pointed out all the trees surrounding the building. They'd probably be in our way.

He's a smart man, Aseyev, and a good commander, one deserving his title, unlike some. I was excited to work with him, to support this effort, and not only because I find counter-offensives extremely interesting. I also just like the man. I like so few people, Yulia.

By late afternoon, we'd carved out sniper trenches in a jagged line along the largest berm near the house, and started our watch. There were four big guns about 1000 meters south of the house, hidden in the trees, and nothing but field between them and the house. We kept our sights on the big guns like hawks on vermin, but there was no action, no targets.

The sun's been down for a while now and we're still in the trenches. It's hard to say when Fritz might attack, so we'll sleep here tonight and keep watch around the clock. A couple of food runners brought us each a canteen of hot stew for dinner, which was greatly appreciated. I credit Aseyev for remembering us in that way. And so I'll say goodnight, Yulia, with a full belly and my rifle at the ready, just as it should be.

28.10.44

I did find some sleep wrapped up in my *plash palatka*, tired as I was from getting up at 2 AM the previous day, and I was reasonably well-rested when I took over the watch from Lida at 4 AM, ready to thrash the Fritzes if they attempted an early morning counter-attack. But the prime time came and went, and it wasn't until afternoon that we spied a line of enemy troops crawling out of the woods, starting across the field, maybe one hundred men. Their guns stood silent, no sign of artillery cover. Was this a suicide mission?

We shot our Bergans first, which Aseyev gave us, to get the feel of them. They're a bit better than the Mosinas at close range. But gods! They take forever to reload, and hold only one round. We switched over to our Mosinas, and shot tracer cartridges at the crawling figures, watching the bullets flash off their helmets. When they reached 100 meters, we switched back to the Bergans and let them have it, shooting and reloading, shooting and reloading. They stood to full height at about 70 meters, and charged at us, and we shot like crazy. They fell like paper cards over the course of a few minutes; I got nine definite kills, and as a platoon we took down at least sixty Fritz. Suddenly, the big guns in the forest came alive and we were peppered with mortar fire. They were all over the place — aiming for our big guns, for our trenches — we weren't sure what they were targeting. Mortars soared over our heads and crashed into the ground near us, then a handful of Fritz ran toward us, bayonets out, yelling their heads off. Everyone was rattled, but we held on and continued to shoot, and we got most of them. When the few that were left got within twenty meters of our trenches, I gave the order and we ran for our lives toward the woods where the artillery guys were positioned.

We all made it out, thank the gods. Our guns had paused when they saw us coming toward them, but they opened fire again as soon as we were behind the line, while the girls and I picked off the Germans that reached our trench line and were attempting to breach the hill. I had just shot another Fritz, and was reloading my rifle, when Aseyev was hit with a mortar shell, ten feet to my right, and was blasted five feet into the air! So fast, our powerful commander was gone. But there was no time to think about that.

Our guns were the clear target now, and every person in that stretch of wood was in danger. I wanted to shoot, but no more Germans came over the hill, and there was no work for my rifle. The gunners continued to fire, but with Aseyev gone, we were untethered. What to do?

A Nazi mortar exploded into gun three, destroying it and the four guys who worked it, and Aseyev's second-in-command shouted "Retreat!"

I heard the order with complete shock. Were we losing this fight? How could we retreat? It was treason! We could be shot by our troops on the way back to base. I wanted so badly to tell my girls, "Keep your position!" but I held my tongue. This man was my superior officer, even if he was wrong. I wanted to stay and fight, because wouldn't it be better to be shot by a Nazi than a red soldier? But we couldn't do it alone, and some of the girls had already started to run back, so I followed.

We ran the first kilometer, then walked toward regimental headquarters, marching solemnly through the dusk, wondering how we would be greeted. I noticed blood on my trousers and wondered if it was Aseyev's. Horopov will be upset to hear of his death — they were great friends.

We saw camp on the horizon, its tents and troops lit up brilliantly in the orange-gold of the setting sun, and an agitation began to brew amongst the girls. We'd done the one thing we're never supposed to do — we left the field of battle to the enemy. Yes, we'd been following orders, but did that matter? Would we be shot by our own comrades?

Some trucks nosed over the hill in front of us, and I thought, *They're coming for us!* But then I saw they were *Katyushas*, a whole battery of then, heading toward the enemy. We clapped and whistled as they motored past, like knights in shining armor. They would destroy the enemy camps, and we'd be saved!

A truck went past with Sasha's new boyfriend, Vovka Emalyanov, riding on top, and Sasha began to jump and cheer, and started singing "Katyusha." I joined in eagerly, pushing past the lump in my throat, and then we were all singing, and clapping, overjoyed that we were saved, when two minutes before we'd been failures, faced with possible death.

> *By the river, Katyusha sang a love song*
> *Of her hero, in a distant land.*
> *Of the one she'd dearly loved for so long,*
> *Holding tight his letters in her hand.*

There were four trucks in the battery, and they set up on the edge of the forest, facing southwest, about twenty meters apart. The *Katyushniks* quickly loaded up the rockets, fourteen in each launcher.

Almost as one, the commanders cranked the remote switch that controlled their launchers, and each rocket roared like a dragon. They spat a line of fire behind them that consumed the grass and scorched the earth within twenty feet. The dreadful wail of the *Katyusha*, so feared by the Germans, filled our ears, a metallic howl like an air-raid siren played on a church organ, as the rockets burst into the sky, and soared toward the enemy, a mob of fifty-six missiles announcing their authority, shutting out the moon and the hopes of the fascists, and casting glorious arcs of white thread through the night sky.

> *Oh, you song, song of a young maiden,*
> *Fly toward the brightly shining stars.*
> *Reach the soldier on the distant border*
> *Bring him Katyusha's love from afar.*

We finished our song as the rockets reached the tail end of their arcs, and watched in silent awe as they slammed into the woods where the enemy was camped and everything went up in flames. Total annihilation.

"*Ypa!*" I cried, and grabbed Sasha in a big hug.

The fire control crews hustled forward to spray the burning ground, as the *Katyushniks* piled onto the backs of the trucks. They moved out quickly, their cargo trucks trailing behind like faithful dogs.

Everything went quiet after that, and it became important to hurry away from where the rockets had been launched.

"Forward!" came from the second-in-command, so the girls and I ran back toward the estate, and then crept back into our trenches to scope out what was happening. Lida and I found a couple of dead Fritz hanging over the side of our trench, but we ignored them and trained our six-folds to the south. No movement, only fires burning everywhere, and the guns had been blown into metal shards.

We watched the area closely for an hour, then I radioed back to give the all-clear, and called for the girls to come out. We made our way down to the great house, where the front door stood gaping open.

"The house is welcoming us," Lida cried, and we all laughed like this was the most hysterical thing we'd ever heard, and marched confidently through the door, proud to be the first of the company to occupy the house.

Inside, I halted in shock. Such splendor! Everything was finer than anything I'd ever seen. The walls and floors were constructed of sleek, dark wood, the linen drapes hung heavy, there was an elegant chandelier, and a huge piano. I went upstairs with some of the others and raided the wardrobes, hoping for some clean underwear. We were lucky in that respect, since we were probably the first females in the house since the owners left, but beyond underthings we were disappointed to find only some very fine dresses. In the end, we took those as well. They were light, and we would cut them up later to use as rags, or as wrappings for our legs.

As we explored the house and found each new room a wonderland of finery, my confusion and anger for these rich Germans grew stronger. "Why invade our land, when they have so much?" Kali asked, wide-eyed. I thought that was a great question. What else could they possibly need?

The beds were all dressed in eiderdown, which I had heard of but never seen. Kali and I lied down on one of the beds and almost didn't get back up again. So comfortable! Like floating in a cloud. But we weren't allowed to sleep there—the softest beds always go to the officers. But we scavenged some pillows and found a parlor with a thick carpet that was large enough to sleep all of us. As we made up our beds, we chatted and laughed, giddy to be alive and spending the night within four solid walls.

Now everyone sleeps except for me. I can't calm down from our big day of fighting. Sasha went to Vovka, her new boyfriend, and I'm fine with that. She might as well claim her happiness while she can. I miss Misha, and the comfort of his warm body at night.

2.Nov.44
Divisional camp at Pillkallen

I've had no time to write, things have been so crazy. It seems like a whole year has gone by in the last few days. That first night in the house, when we were all fast asleep on our plush carpet, the Nazis launched a surprise attack, just like at Kozie Gory. We were jolted from our sleep by gunshots firing off somewhere in the house, and jumped instantly to our feet and grabbed our rifles. Peering out the window, I saw several Fritz crawling up the southern hill toward the house. There was more gunfire from downstairs, and then, with mounting dread, we heard a high-pitched metallic whistle coming toward us, and the barn exploded. Some of the artillery guys had been sleeping in that barn! Now gone!

We were in serious danger, and the girls panicked. "Stand your ground!" I yelled, but this time they didn't listen, they all grabbed their rucksacks and fled. Only Kali stayed. She was the only brave one. Together, Kali and I shot from the windows at the targets we could get through the trees, picking them off one by one.

And then there were no more crawling Fritzes. We looked at each other and listened hard to the sounds from the house. We didn't hear any more gunfire, and no more flying mortars either. Were we clear to leave, or was the enemy in the house, lying in wait for us? We sat absolutely still for what seemed like forever, but was probably thirty minutes, our ears pressed to the door, listening hard. There were voices from the floor below, and I thought they were Russian, but couldn't be sure.

Slowly, quietly, we crept down the stairs, and when we reached the first floor, we relaxed our defenses, hearing that the voices were certainly Russian. The Nazi sneak attack had not succeeded—we still had the house.

But what had become of the rest of our unit? We went looking for them, and stopped in horror outside the back door. Lida Vdovina lay across the steps, clearly dead. Her throat had been slashed so deeply that her head hung back off the steps at a gruesome angle, her eyes open wide and staring.

"Oh God," Kali moaned, and dropped to her knees next to the corpse.

I put my hands over my face and felt my throat close up. Lida, my friend, my partner, dead! How could it be?

Maybe there was some mistake, maybe she was alive. Struggling to breathe, I knelt in Lida's blood, next to Kali, and forced myself to look at her clearly. Those staring eyes, the deep stillness of the body. Dead. Lida was gone.

Tears came fast and hard. Because Lida didn't deserve to die, Yulia. There's always a chance, death looms over all of us at war, but Lida was so good! *Why* did the girls run away? Lida would be alive, they'd all be alive, if only they'd stayed with me and Kali!

And where were the others? I looked around wildly, half-expecting to see the entire platoon lying dead on the grounds, but saw only a couple of dead Fritzes, and Kali, vomiting off the other side of the steps.

"Oh Kali," I said, "is this my fault?"

She turned and looked at me, wiping her mouth on her sleeve. "Don't you dare, Roza," she hissed. "The Nazis have done this, not you! We are at WAR. People die."

I breathed deeply and nodded, trying to pull my face back into a mask of neutrality. "What happened here?" I wondered, with only a trace of a tremor in my voice.

We learned later that while Kali and I were busy shooting at the fascists, the girls had been involved in their own fight as they fled the house, with a handful of Fritz who had gotten around to the back entrance. Lida, who was last out the door, was ambushed and killed instantly. Two other girls were slashed with bayonets, but fought off the attackers and were not so wounded that they couldn't walk, so everyone fled back to headquarters, leaving Lida's body to be fetched later.

This is the first time one of my own troops has been killed, and that it should have been Lida! It's terrible in every way, Yulia. In my heart of hearts, I'd rather it had been me.

Kali and I would bury Lida — we didn't even need to discuss it. We chose the prettiest spot we could find in the dark, under a tree not far from the house, and used our trench tools to dig the hole. We closed her eyes, and taped her head back into its proper place, and I tied my blue scarf around the bandage. Then we lowered her into the ground and covered her with dirt, both crying the whole time. I scratched her name onto a rock with my *finka* and placed it on top, so that she could be found by her family, or anyone wanting to look for her.

Kali and I held hands as we stood looking at the grave.

"Lida, you were a good friend," Kali said.

"A great friend," I said, "and a great soldier. I'm so sorry, Lida. I'll miss you every day."

"Rest in peace," Kali whispered.

We stood there a few more moments, until Kali muttered that we should get out of sight since there were very likely Germans in the area. We hadn't cared about that while we were taking care of Lida's body, but Kali was right — it was time to go. We went to fetch our rucksacks from the back steps, when the slightest flash of gold caught my eye, and crouching down, I saw that it was a small gold cross on a broken chain. Lida's cross. I picked it up and wrapped my fingers around it.

We got our packs and made the long trek back to base camp in silence. I cried the whole way, letting my grief out in the dark. I was so sorry, and so afraid to face the other girls, afraid that they would blame me for Lida's death. I thought they would pile onto me hard, but no one said anything. And why not? This time I almost wanted their anger.

Lida Vdovina was a really good person, a simple person, always ready to help. An accomplished sniper, who'd argued with me for a chance to take down that German sniper. She loved her mama, and her horse Freya back home. She was keen to serve her country. I will carry her cross in my pocket, as a reminder.

As I'm writing this now, I don't see Lida as she was in life. I see her as I saw her last—lying in the dirt with my blue scarf wrapped around her neck.

At least she died quickly.

We found Sasha at camp, who felt terrible for having been off with Vovka during the ambush. I covered for her, so at least she didn't need to add to her worries by getting into trouble with regimental command.

In the end, the platoon made a good impression on the top brass, but the price was too dear, with Lida dead, not to mention Aseyev. Kali was put forward for the Order of Courage, and I for my third Order of Glory. I hope I don't get it. Hard to think of becoming a Full Cavalier on the back of Lida's death. The one thing I will take away from this mission is the resolve to never again bring the entire platoon with me into combat. It's more natural to split up anyway, really. Not often that someone wants an entire platoon of snipers.

The platoon is down to eleven now, with Lida dead, and Anna and Dusya wounded in the hospital. Tomorrow we head home, and Misha should be back from his mission, so I'll get to see him.

2.Nov.44

Made the long drive back to our billet today, eager to see Misha, but no Misha to be seen. More disappointment, but the holidays are coming, so he'll be back soon. Lida will never be back.

Lots of mail had come while we were gone to Pillkallen, including the November edition of *Frontline Humor* with my picture on the cover. The image was nothing special, it made me look about twelve years old, but no matter how I look these photos and articles are followed by a slew of letters and invitations from men. People can't seem to resist fame or celebrity or something. Am I really a celebrity, Yulia? It seems so strange. I wonder if you have seen any of these newspapers or magazines. What have I done differently from any other Soviet soldier, except run away to the Front? Yet I receive such praise!

Ilya Ehrenburg wrote about me in the Moscow paper: "Let the Russian mother rejoice who gave birth to, brought up and gave this glorious, noble daughter to the Motherland! Yesterday, Sniper Roza Shanina in a single outing exterminated five Nazis. Congratulations on your military achievements, Comrade Shanina! The personal tally of this fearless young woman is now fifty-one dead Hitlerites and three she has personally taken prisoner."

This feels like glory, Yulia, but Lida deserved it as well. There was no mention of her. Does running away to the Front and fighting hard set me apart somehow? I will choose to believe that it's my fighting spirit receiving this praise. It's true that I got five Nazis in one outing, and more than a few times, and I did bring in three prisoners by myself. I did earn two Medals of Glory, and have been put forward for another. I've been willing to go on the attack, always, when others have held back, but Lida never did. She was a good, dutiful soldier, who received no mention when she was slaughtered by the Nazis. Why am I the hero? Do you suppose that hero*s know* that they are heroes?

8 November 1944

October Revolution Day has come and gone, and we've done a lot of celebrating and a little work—just some patrols. I had loads of invitations to parties at other regiments, but I was only interested in going by Malchonov. I thought he'd have interesting people around him, but really I wanted to know what was happening with Sergei. I haven't heard anything in ages, Yulia! But Misha really wanted to stay home ("Better to be with good friends on a holiday,") so I agreed and sent a note off to Pyotr, asking him to come for a visit.

We went to the local celebration, and the party was swinging when we walked in, with two guys playing accordion on stage, and a singer wearing a fancy red dress. And food! I haven't seen so much food in ages, and plenty of vodka everywhere. It was a mash up, we were herring in a barrel, and had some trouble slipping through the crowd to the long table that was heavy with dishes, including *blini*,[44] *kolach*,[45] and *vereniki*,[46] and a mouth-watering *korovai*.[47] I was stuffing my face with *cepelinai*,[48] my favorite local food, when I spotted Sasha and Kali not far off.

I snuck up behind Sasha and grabbed her shoulders.

"Roza," she cried. "Come meet the pilots of the 885th!"

Sasha looked flushed and happy, and I suspected her vodka glass had been refilled a couple of times already. I looked around the table and saw that she and Kali were surrounded by good-looking men I'd never seen before.

"Where's Vovka?" I asked.

Sasha's expression morphed into anger. "With the devil, for all I care."

---

[44] *Blini*—little pancakes.

[45] *Kolach*—Ukrainian word for lightly sweet bread often served at celebrations.

[46] *Vereniki*—Russian name for dumplings (i.e. pierogi, pelmeni).

[47] *Korovai*—an ancient celebration bread often served at weddings, symbolizing good luck and prosperity.

[48] *Cepelinai*—potato dumplings stuffed with meat and rice, often described as the national dish of Lithuania.

I glanced at Kali—she raised her eyebrows and looked away. A moment later she was introducing me to the pilots at the table, and budging over to make room for me to sit down.

I looked around and saw Misha coming toward me, so I squeezed in next to Kali and nodded at the strangers. Someone handed me a glass of vodka, and the man across the table offered me a cigarette. I accepted it from him, and he said, "You are Roza Shanina, the famous deadly sniper."

I shrugged, and smiled, and gestured to Misha, now standing behind me. "And this is my boyfriend, Misha Panarin."

"Lucky man!"

"And you are?" Misha asked.

"Nikolai Shevchenko," he said, handing a glass to Misha.

Another Nikolai, I thought. "Nastrovia, Nikolai," I said. We clinked glasses and downed the vodka in one swallow. It was good, real vodka, not the pigswill that the soldiers drink to get drunk.

We must have been there for hours, drinking with Shevchenko and his friends and Sasha and Kali. It felt good to let loose, and I was definitely drunk, but not so bad that I couldn't light a cigarette. At one point Kali stood up and toasted Lida with tears rolling down her face, and Sasha and I fell over her, crying. Shortly after that, I got up to straighten myself out and use the latrine and found myself face-to-face with Gudkov, the odd little man who took me on my first plane ride. He looked at me so sternly. He'd written me a bunch of letters, at least four of them, but I never responded, and he seemed to want to yell at me about that. Did he expect an apology, or did he think he deserved some attention from me? That wasn't going to happen, Yulia, because I was certain that I owed him nothing, and skirted around him to go outside. Even if I didn't find the man strange and creepy, I would forever remember his smugness about Sergei.

My vodka glass was somehow always full, and we were all getting steadily drunk even though we ate a good dinner. Misha went missing, and I remember getting up from the table to look for him, and falling back down into my seat. After that, the next thing I remember was waking up this morning, not sure where I was, a man in bed with me, pressed up to me, with his arm wrapped around my waist. *Misha*, I thought lazily, happily, and then I realized it wasn't Misha. Lord, Yulia, I can't describe the horrible feeling in my stomach, and not just from the hangover. *What had I done?*

Coming fully awake, my first feeling was relief when I found that I was still wearing my uniform. *Maybe not so bad.* Next, I became aware that my head was pounding and my stomach swirling. I needed to get outside, and quickly.

I carefully lifted the man's arm off of me, scooted out from under it, and bolted out of the dugout. I had barely hit the cold morning air when my stomach contracted and sent acid spewing onto a nearby tree. I leaned against the tree, moaning, my heart throbbing in my temples. *Just kill me now.*

"Roza?"

I turned to the voice and saw Nikolai Schevchenko emerging from the bunker, his hair sticking up at odd angles.

"What happened last night?" he asked, rubbing his face.

I started to reply but my stomach lurched, and I vomited again, leaning against the tree. After a minute or two I stood up and faced Schevchenko.

"Too much vodka," was all I could think to say.

Schevchenko nodded. He looked around, seeming unsure what to do. "Nice to meet you," he said, and stumbled away.

I watched him go and wondered what exactly had happened that had landed him in my bed. I was pretty sure we didn't fool around, because we were both wearing our clothes and both had been dead drunk. Groaning with embarrassment, I walked into the woods for better privacy, pulled out my dagger, and said a few words over it, to remind myself who I was.

I don't remember exactly what I said, but it was along the lines of promising myself that I'd never again get so drunk that I could end up in bed with a strange man, that Misha was my one true love, that no other man would touch me. It was silly, but I felt better afterwards.

Nobody said a thing to me today about Shevchenko, and the man seems to have disappeared. Maybe I'll be lucky and no one will know about my mistake.

15.Nov.44

Nights have been dead cold, and we have the worst bunker in the regiment. It's always this way for the females — the oldest, coldest and moldiest. Most of the girls sleep elsewhere, with their boyfriends, or in the worst case, with any man willing to take them into their warm dugout. Even I, who am accustomed to the cold of the north, can't stay warm enough in our bunker to actually sleep. I've been staying with Misha in the artillery guys' bunker next to the Front, since Ferdinand doesn't stay warm unless the engine's running.

This morning, when I stopped by my platoon's bunker, I saw that not a single girl had spent the night there. The situation is infuriating, Yulia. How dare they put us in a situation that is not livable, in which we are forced for survival to seek mens' warmer beds, and then call us "army whores?" Add to this, and I'm sorry to say this, sweet sister, but two nights ago, one of my snipers was violated by General Kazaryan, when she and two other girls had been sent to support his division for a couple of days. She tried to fight him off but was overpowered, and actually locked into his bunker. And she, in a strong love relationship, was devastated, saying "My life is over, I am no longer a *devotchka*."

I'm told it's better for female soldiers now than it was at the start of the war, but truly, assaults can and do happen. I am protected somewhat, not only by Misha, but because a lot of people recognize me and think I'm famous or something. The other girls have it worse, and who do you think are the real offenders? The top brass. But that's no surprise. There's a brutal kind of aggression that comes with power. *Kings forget they are men*, Misha says, and he's right.

Pyotr Malchnov came by for a visit yesterday, but didn't have anything for me from Sergei. God, I hope he isn't bereft. I haven't given up hope that Papa will do something. I suppose I'll have to write to you to beg for information, if only in code.

12 November 1944

I was called up today before General Kazaryan and criticized for my platoon's poor discipline, lack of patrols and absences during the holiday celebrations. I could hardly look at the man, knowing what he'd done to my friend, but I kept my face neutral and forced myself to look at the middle of his chest.

It was true that work slacked off over the holidays, but not just with my platoon, it was the whole regiment. There was an unspoken agreement to have a real holiday. We did do patrols, which was more than other units did, and it burned to be chastised by this terrible man for not doing patrols, when we actually did our job and what did he do? Abused his power at a nice girl's expense. Not as bad as Sergei's boss, but still—bad! But I took the reprimand without comment, because there was no way I could say to him what I really wanted to say.

More articles and photographs of me came out this week. I've given up being worried about Stalin watching me. War is the greater danger, to be sure. But I'm beginning to be pestered by admirers wherever I go, and it's really distracting. It makes me self-conscious, like I'm always on stage. I was happy to get letters from the preschool in Arkhangelsk. Some of my former students wrote me notes, praising their "favorite teacher, so strong and brave." I get letters from total strangers almost every day, mostly guys in the army telling me that they've seen my picture in the *Crocodile* or some other place, asking me to send a photo. The letters I like best come from civilians, both male and female, expressing respect and thanks for my work.

When I think that my family and friends have seen and read these articles—no one can know how much it means to me. The critic in me, that dark voice deep inside, remembers what Blokhin said to Misha that day—Stalin likes my pretty face—and I fear that's why I'm receiving such glory. I didn't do anything to get this face, I was born with it. But my kill count speaks for itself, right? Highest in the platoon, and unusually high for seven months of service.

If I'm being completely honest, my passion comes from a flaw within me. I can't stand to be idle, I must have action around me to be comfortable. I have no control over it, Yulia. This is my greatest weakness, perhaps, and it's also the reason my kill count is highest amongst the snipers. I guess everyone has weaknesses, but it seems strange for my courage to come from a flaw.

"Perhaps strength does come from weakness," Misha said, as we sat in Ferdinand's cab, looking at the latest write-up about me in the newspaper.

Fifty-seven times in succession, thank her, thousands of Soviet lives she's saved. —Ilya Ehrenburg

"Maybe it's a balancing thing," he said.

"But is it real strength? If it grows out of weakness?"

"I don't think it's one-way. Weakness could also grow from strength." He looked up from the paper. "But strength is strength, wherever it comes from, right? For you—you need to be in the middle of the action, whether you were born that way or something happened to you, I don't know. But you are that way, and it makes you fearless. And since you're also incredibly capable, and smart, fast, athletic… we get you—an amazing soldier."

I grabbed his hand. "So you accept it now, you understand that I'm not trying to die?"

He smiled, but there was something else in his eyes, like sadness or resignation. "Yes, I understand," he said.

I pulled myself into his lap and kissed him.

"But I'm sure they put you in the papers because you're so much fun to look at," he said, inches away from my mouth.

I lurched away from him and smacked him on the shoulder. After all those nice things he said!

"Oy," Misha said, grinning. "Come back here, Unseen Terror of the Eastern Front. You've got killer eyes you know, in more ways than one."

What a Misha! Makes me feel heavy and light at the same time. I love that he does that, so much, Yulia. But things have changed since Lida died. It's like something in me died a little bit too. We're still together every night, but I'm not completely there.

All this praise… I feel guilty, because I'm not the only one who deserves it, and probably there are others more deserving. What is the nature of glory anyway? Golubov says glory is "to split the enemy's skull, or have your own skull split in defense of the Motherland." If that's true, I do deserve it, and the real problem is not that I'm being praised, but that others aren't. Or will this come at a price that I don't yet see?

23.Nov.44
Western Lithuania

I got called to divisional headquarters for an interview, and to meet some generals. I was there for two days, and when I got back last night, I found Sasha and Kali waiting for me. They pulled me into the woods and told me that the artillery guns had been targeted in a mess of cannon fire and Misha had been blown up.

I didn't believe it, Yulia. How many times have I gone down the road of thinking Misha was dead? And it's never been true.

"Where's his body?" I wanted to know. And what do you think? No body, Yulia! "He's not dead," I said. Sasha gave me a teary look and Kali said I should speak with Kolya, who'd seen the whole thing.

Kolya "saw Ferdinand go up in flames" along with a lot of other guns, "a massive explosion," "no way those guys made it out."

"Are you sure he was there," I asked.

"Where else would he be?" came the answer.

But nobody actually saw him get killed, and there's no body! He could be lying in the woods, wounded. I decided to go to him and started to walk out that instant, but Sasha and Kali were there, holding me back.

"You'd be walking into a German camp!"

"What do I care about that?"

"It's suicide, Roza! Is that what you want?"

"Misha is what I want!" I cried. "I want Misha…"

Sasha began to cry again and wrapped her arms around me. I leaned against her for a moment, but then broke free and ran back to our billet, back to my bed.

They all think he's dead, Yulia, but how can that be? How can my Misha be dead? He was so much better than me at everything, so much better than anybody! I always thought if one of us were to die, it would be me. I'm reckless, where he's careful, methodical. He's so smart, Yulia, and I'm, well I'm not stupid, but Misha is brilliant. He can't be dead.

But Lida died, and she was very good.

How will I know the truth with no body? Oh God. Can I do this?

25.Nov.44

Lying here like a slug for three hours now, in my own freezing cold bunk. Did not go with the girls to the trenches today or yesterday. What is the point in getting out of bed, walking around, putting food in my mouth, shooting my gun?

I'm filled with blackness. Not in some metaphorical sense—it's as if the inside of my body is really filled with a black mass, a mass as black as outer space, full of vast galaxies of nothingness.

This rock that we stand on, that we call Earth, it feels so solid beneath our feet, but it's always spinning, spinning through vast nothingness in a never-ending circle, churning out birth and death. And none of us can escape the cycle—none of us will get out of here alive.

But I can't think of him as a corpse, like Lida, with dead eyes and gray skin.

Last night, he came to me in a dream. I was alone, walking along an unfamiliar riverbank that I somehow knew was the Dvina. It was cold and wet, with a sharp wind that pushed right through me, and I wore only camouflage. I walked quickly, like I had somewhere to get to in a hurry, although it wasn't clear where that was, when Misha called out to me. I stopped and looked around, and there he was, on the other side of the river. The grass was green over there, the sun shining. Misha looked perfect, and he was smiling at me from across twenty meters of rushing water.

"Misha!" I cried, and started into the stream, but the river was powerful, and deep, and I couldn't cross.

Suddenly he was right next me, in the rain, pulling me back onto the river bank. He put his arms around me and I realized the blackness was gone. We held each other for a long time, long enough for me to feel our love surrounding us, warm as a cocoon in the middle of a rainstorm.

"Roza," he said, at last. "Keep going. It's my turn to be scout."

And with one last caress, he was gone, and I woke up in the freezing bunker. I curled up in a ball and cried my eyes out, until the blackness came back and chased the feelings away.

They are hovering somewhere in the air, my feelings, like they've been cut from my body, and when I look at them, they seem foreign, like they belong to someone else.

Time conquers all, and one day will conquer me, and my black soul. What do I need now? What am I good for?

27.Nov.44
A hole in the ground, unfit for a pig, western Lithuania

The platoon got transferred to the 203rd and I was forced to drag myself out of bed, pack up and put one foot in front of the other on a long march. Afterward, I felt a little better, but when we arrived, we found ourselves once again assigned to sleep in filthy, freezing holes in the ground. When I complained, the captain said "Why give you good quarters when none of you will sleep there?" which is a fair point, but also totally unfair. "You're killing me," I said, and he just snorted. I watched the girls race each other out of the dugout to find the men with warm beds and secure their night's sleep, while Kali and I stayed behind, shaking our heads and writing letters.

Now everyone is going to bed with everyone, trading partners. More fodder for thinking all female soldiers are *zchenchinas*, and I'm frustrated with the girls. I find myself agreeing with Kali — "How can you fight against something if you accept it?" There must be another way to stay warm. They're taking the easy path. And these men — some of whom I consider friends — take their advantage. It's more betrayal, all around, but there isn't anything I can do about it.

At least we're closer to the Front now. I want to get back into combat, whether it cures me or kills me.

I miss Sasha, who I've been avoiding because every time she looks at me, it seems like she's about to cry. Kali is good, but I've missed our Stray Troika, my family at the Front. It's been very hard, with no Misha, and no Sasha and Kali. This morning, Sasha sought me out in the field kitchen and sat on the ground next to me with her bowl of *kasha*. She wasn't crying this time — she was eager to tell me about a dream she'd had last night.

In Sasha's dream, she, Kali and I walked together in Gorky Park, two years after the war ended. It was a beautiful, sunny day, and Moscow was back to its former bustling self. We were students at the university, spending a Sunday outdoors, deciding our destination as we walked, when we came upon a slender young man in uniform, elegantly dressed, with a baby in his arms, a slim brunette girl beside him. They smiled and chatted with each other. This man turned his gaze upon us and we recognized him, a *Katyushnik* from our time at war. In that moment, the past front-line friendship of the *Katyushniks* and snipers passed between us, and we nodded to each other, and the family walked on. Two years of peace had so changed everything, we had all gotten beyond the hardships of war and didn't want to revisit it. The three of us walked on, but Sasha felt sad, hurt by this encounter, because the man had been Toska, who she'd once been so close to, now a stranger in the street. That was the end of her dream.

I don't know why Sasha shared this dream with me, but it made me feel better. "Life goes on," she said, "and things that seem so heavy now will lighten up," but that our Troika will last beyond this war experience, and that we need to stick together. I think she must be right.

29.Nov.44, 21:30
Same stink hole, with ice on my bunk

I went to visit Vanya Horopov's regiment today, excited to learn that they were positioned so close to us, but the air was pure fog, the Germans a distant blur on the horizon. I went into a trench and shot a few times, not knowing if I hit a Fritz or a hedgehog or a tree. Hopefully not one of our own. It's hard with this weather — visibility is so bad. I thought we would see more action here, but so far that hasn't been true. We go into the trenches every morning, far from the Front, and we are supposed to keep watch on the distant German camp, but we can see nothing in this fog. Talk about Fog of War—this is the real thing. Today, right on the frontlines, I saw nothing, did nothing, and had no idea where the enemy was.

I'm constantly anxious, it pulses through my temples every instant. I wish I knew why, but I can't handle any pause in the action. It feels like a giant snake has my head clenched in its jaws, the first step toward sucking me into its belly. And now, these past few days, every time I close my eyes, I see Lida's severed head, with its staring eyes. Why now? It's been a month since she died.

While I was gone today, the girls went to the rear lookout post as usual and dropped into the trenches, the fog so thick that you could not see your own hand in front of your face. Such a joke to be on lookout with no visibility, but they went anyway. I reported to Blokhin that I was ill, and thank God for that, or I might have been in real trouble from what happened during my absence.

The girls sat blind in the trenches, fog swirling around them, chatting to pass the time. Suddenly a Nazi reconnaissance group jumped into the trench and grabbed four of our snipers: Anya Nesterova, Lyuba Tanailova, Dusya Kekesheva and Dusya Shambarova. The Germans pulled them from the trench and dragged them across the field toward the enemy camp. Anya and Lyuba shouted out "Open fire!" to our troops, but no one had the heart to shoot blindly into the fog and kill their own comrades. One of the Nazis stepped on a mine; he died in the explosion and Dusya Shambarova was injured. In the confusion, Dusya Kekesheva managed to struggle free and ran back to the trench, while Dusya Shambarova lay in the field with horrible shrapnel wounds from the mine, pretending to be dead, although she managed to crawl back to the trench later. Anya and Lyuba were dragged off, prisoners of the Nazis!

I shudder to think what those girls will face in the hands of the fascists, if they are even alive. They're likely dead. The Germans hate our snipers and kill them instantly when they get one, but it's possible they don't know that Anya and Lyuba are snipers. They wore camouflage, without their sniper medals, so maybe the Germans wouldn't know.

"You couldn't have saved them," Sasha insisted, when I shared that I felt responsible for not being there. "The fog was so thick we had no idea what was happening until it was all over."

Sasha was probably right, but as commander, I always feel guilty, as if everything is my fault. That's just how it works — someone is responsible for everything, good or bad, and it seems to always be the person in charge.

Two more gone, probably dead. I'll write to Malchonov about that.

1.Dec.44, 13:05

The filthy Nazis littered our camp with paper flyers, photographs of Anya and Lyuba splayed across them, with the phrase "Captured!" in huge letters across the bottom. They dropped them from a plane, scattered them all over the place. They were older pictures, standard Red Army stock from when the girls first enlisted, and I wonder where on earth they got them?

I know I shouldn't take myself so seriously, but I do wonder, if I'd been there, would things have ended differently?

What good am I, Yulia, if I keep getting people killed? It should have been me.

6.Dec.44

God and Hell, what a long and dreadful day! I will not forget the sixth of December any time soon, the day my own platoon turned on me, like a pack of wolverines. Kaleriya ran up to Sasha and I on our way home from the *Katyushniks* and warned us that Nastya Mochstenko had roused the troops to confront me, that they were waiting for me in our bunker. I was grateful to Kali for the warning. Hard as it was, it would have been even more difficult as a blind ambush.

Nastya was the leader, and she was supported by Shura, Dusya Krasnoborova, Anya, Dusya Kekesheva, Zina, Zoya and Masha.

"Here comes the *heroine*," Nastya sneered, as I walked into the bunker.

I looked around at their hard-set faces, meeting the eyes of those who were brave enough to look directly at me. "Shura, Zoya, Masha. Aren't you supposed to be on lookout?" I said, direct and business-like. Best that they recognized my authority, whether they liked it or not.

"That's nice," Nastya said, her voice dripping with venom, "you who are never where you're supposed to be, telling us where to go!"

Several of the girls nodded agreement.

"Every day, we go about our duties as we are told," Nastya continued, "while Roza Shanina, the great heroine, does whatever she wants, running to the Front to play with the officers."

"I don't go to the Front to play!"

"It's not just the officers," said Anna, "it's Malchonov she is messing around with. She runs to be with him, and leaves us to do the platoon's dirty work. She never works in the trenches, never checks on us, does nothing for us."

This made me very angry, so angry that I didn't trust myself to speak.

"She goes to bed with all the officers," Nastya interrupted. "She sucks up to them to get a better situation for herself."

"Not true!" I said. "Not even a little true! And if I have a better situation than all of you, why am I the only one sleeping in this cold bunker?"

I felt that this was a good point, that it was proof that they were being unfair, but they ignored it.

"You are a platoon commander, Roza," Masha said, with less heat than the others. "I don't think you should leave so often as you do."

"It's not just the absences," Zoya said coldly. "What about lying about her kill count? She marks down kills even when she doesn't know whether or not she hit her mark."

"Everything about you is a fake," Nastya said, viciously, "and it's your fault that Luyba and Anya were captured, and that Lida was killed. You're a terrible commander, and we aren't going to put up with it any longer. From now on, we won't follow your orders. You're *nothing* to us."

My stomach had dropped to my feet as they accused me of the crimes I've been beating myself up about, but I was also so angry, Yulia, more angry than I can remember ever being.

"What do you think you can do about it? I'm still your commander," I hissed, and spun around to leave.

I crashed into Sasha and Kali, who were standing behind me. They looked as shocked as I felt, and also didn't seem to know what to say. I strode past them, went directly to Degtyarev and reported Nastya, Anna, and Zoya for insubordination. Let's see how they feel about being at odds with their commander.

When I left Degtyarev, I sought out Sasha and Kali, to find out how long the others had been washing my bones behind my back. My friends were aware of some little jealousy, but had no idea that the troops were so angry.

"They're jealous," Sasha said, "and when they see that themselves, they'll be sorry and come asking your forgiveness."

"Jealous of me," I laughed hard, bitterly. "Because my life has been so great, because it's so much better than theirs?"

"They envy your fame, and your authority," Kali said. "Truly, Roza, I don't think anyone believes you've had an easy life, but here, most have it worse than you."

I glared at her, surprised.

"Don't be angry. You must see that the girls can't handle that you're doing better than they are. You're in all the papers and magazines, you're called on to meet generals, you have the highest kill count, and the most handsome boyfriend—"

"Misha is *dead*!"

"Our people can't stand the idea of anyone getting ahead," Kali pushed on. "Really, I think almost anyone would rather pull a person down to their level, rather than see them do more or have more."

Now, after brooding about the situation all afternoon and night, with bruised feelings, I think Kali was right. This is yet another hazard of leadership. Going forward, I will not sink to their level of throwing around accusations, and instead I will become the perfect platoon commander, watching over them closely in the trenches. I will never say about them what they said about me, but where in the past I had turned a friendly eye away from the girls' imperfections in their duties, now I will shine a light on these problems. And if I go to the Front, I will take extra precautions so that they won't know. What they don't know won't hurt them.

So funny, that the girls are jealous of my authority, when I would be pleased to rid myself of being platoon commander. I've been asking the top brass to make someone else commander for some time now. Not that I haven't liked my post—I like it fine. But I'm not free to come and go as I would if I were not commander. They are jealous of something that has no value for me. I'd be thrilled to give up command of this platoon if I could serve almost anywhere on the Front, or even be assigned as a regular sniper with one of the forward companies. I would give up anything, even my life, to go on the attack, but so far, I can't get anyone to listen to me.

If I'd been born a boy, no one would pay attention to where I went and what I did, and I wouldn't have to flash my dagger at the guys who look at me like hungry wolves. If I were a boy, I wouldn't have to lie to myself and everyone else that I'm still a *devotchka*. I wouldn't have to deal with being called a *zenschina*. Isn't it amazing, that even women who are raped are called *zenschinas*? Where is the truth in that, Yulia? A girl can be the picture of modesty and still be thought a whore, simply because she's in the army. I know that I'm not a whore, but to say I've been modest is a stretch. How can one be modest at war? I wonder how it would be if the roles were reversed, and girls could go to bed with anyone they wanted, with men being afraid for their reputations. Ha! When a lobster whistles on top of a mountain. It's all twisted up.

Nastya doesn't believe that I've killed as many Fritz as I get credit for. In my defense, there are times when I shoot at a lot of targets in the dark, and it's hard to tell if it was a kill or not, and I don't claim those kills, although some of my bullets surely hit their mark. If a Fritz is standing, I target him accurately, and I get the kill. Those ones count. In most cases, I'm shooting at stationary targets or marching soldiers, and I know if I've hit them. I keep an accurate tally of those hits. Deserters are hard, and I will aim to scare, not kill. I have no deserter kills. I know that my count isn't perfectly accurate, but to say it's a lie—not fair! I have almost certainly killed *more* than my tally suggests.

On the attack, we must shoot precisely at close range, and not miss, or we will be killed. The last counter-attack I went on with the guys, they wanted to test my accuracy. I was the only one shooting, while they watched, and I took down fifteen Fritz, maybe more. "Well done," they said. Because I'm good, Yulia.

On defense, I often shoot from fifty meters at standing targets, and hit them square in the chest. I've killed 57 Fritz on defense, not one of them an assigned target. Let the girls talk. I know that I've taken down more than my kill count would suggest.

I crave a fight, a fierce fight. I'd give anything to go and fight with the soldiers on the frontlines this minute. If I were a boy, it would be allowed. The urge torments me, so strong that most nights I cannot sleep. It's like an addiction. There are those who need vodka — I need combat. This is my weakness, why I abandon my platoon. But isn't it also a strength, out here? Oh God, why do I have this mysterious nature? Right or wrong, I don't like that it controls me.

Thank the gods for Sasha and Kali, my good friends. Sasha, Kali and I, we all had one year at the institute, and have very different personalities, but we're close, we're good comrades, and I respect them more than anyone else in the platoon. Life is easier with friends, and I've grown used to them. I'm bored without them. Kaleriya is a good girl, she has no ego and a bold, very rational mind, well-versed in all matters, and a golden memory. Sasha is the sweet, girlish girl. Sasha, Kali and I — us friendly Stray Troika. At least they understand me.

I feel better for writing it all out, but it's sapped my energy. Must sleep, my dear Yulia. I hope you know how much I love you, and that I could never be jealous of any good that comes your way.

FOURTH JOURNAL:
WINTER

13.Dec.44
Field hospital

Two nights ago, I dreamed that my right shoulder was injured, that I couldn't use my arm to shoot my rifle. Then yesterday, as I was working in the lookout trench, I felt a pain in that shoulder, remembered my dream, and next thing I knew I'd been shot twice in that same spot. Two feet to the right or left and I'd have been fine, but luck put two bullets into my right shoulder, and somehow I knew it would happen, Yulia, which is the strange thing about this. What can it mean, that I would see the injury in a dream before it happened? So amazing, but not frightening. My dreams have been such friends to me. I'm glad for anything to help me believe they are real, because it opens the door to other possibilities. How can we know what is really out there? Maybe something beautiful, something like what my dreams have shown me.

I'm laid up at the field hospital, because although the wound didn't hurt badly, my friends forced me to come here, where the medics dug out the bullets. Now, my shoulder feels like it's on fire, the pain from the operation so much greater than the pain from the injury. I can still write, but it's difficult. I don't think I could shoot today, but hopefully I'll be back at the Front soon. The monster in my chest roars for action, but the nurse says it will take a month to heal. I can't tell you how much I hate hearing this. A month of laying in bed! I'll be crazy long before an entire month goes by.

15.Dec.44
Still in the field hospital

Nurse Katya tells me that I will be moved to the rest home near Smolensk today or tomorrow. I'm *not* eager for this to happen. My shoulder feels much better, almost perfect really. I asked to be released to the Front but the doctor would not allow it.

"Sergeant Shanina, you must rest," he said.

"If I could stay and recover here, in the field hospital, I could command a company from here, while I'm recovering," I suggested.

"I cannot allow it. There will be plenty of war for you when you have healed."

This was so disappointing, so infuriating! I loathe the condescension that seems to thrive inside every Soviet man. I may run away. It has worked for me in the past.

Nurse Katya asked me if I have a boyfriend on the Front.

"I have no one," I said. It made me sad to say so, because I realized it was true. But she just winked at me and shook her head.

She didn't believe me, and how typical. She's very girlish, probably unable to see how anyone would be eager to go to the frontlines. I'd like to tell her how Sasha, who likes ribbons and dresses as much as anyone, fights like a warrior. I'm sure it's easier for her to believe that I can't bear to be separated from my lover for a couple of weeks, but I have no one at the Front. Truly, I just want to be back in the fight. That monster in my chest won't let me be comfortable in my own skin unless I'm in the thick of combat.

25.Dec.44
Army rest home, near Smolensk

I was pleased to have a visitor today—Pyotr Malchonov! It's been such a long time since we've met, and I've missed our conversations.

I was taking my time with my *kasha* this morning when Pyotr arrived. It was an especially good *kasha*, with fresh cloudberries—a real treat. But I was feeling low after brooding about all of the bad things that happened last month, and I was waiting for my appetite to appear so that the good kasha wouldn't go to waste.

I was pondering the idea that the *ends justify the means*, and just beginning to fume, wondering what Communist ideal could possibly be served by overpowering and raping a woman, when Pyotr stuck his long nose in front of mine.

"No greeting for your old friend?" he asked.

"Pyotr!" I jumped up and threw my good arm open wide.

He laughed, hugged me gruffly and kissed my left cheek, and swung into a white metal chair across from my spot at the table.

"What are you doing here?"

"I was passing through Smolensk and came to visit my favorite sniper," he said. "How are you? Are they going to set you free soon?"

"Who can say? They don't tell me their plans. But it can't be much longer, I think I'm basically healed," I said, trying to curb the whine of resentment that I heard in my voice.

"Good news! I imagine you've been going crazy in here. You were looking far too serious just now as I walked in."

"Yes, well, you know how that goes. Give me some free time and I'll find my way into the dark corners of my mind."

"*Da*, I do know," he nodded. "Maybe that's why we like each other. But is that why you're always eager for action? To avoid the need to think?"

"That's part of it," I agreed, an idea coming over me. Here was my good friend, a powerful journalist, a man who had a voice with the public. "Let me get you some tea and we can have a nice long visit."

I begged some tea and *kasha* for Pyotr and we settled in to our breakfasts. The buckwheat and cloudberries were delicious, and with each bite I became more convinced that my idea was a good one. But I let Pyotr finish his food before I would ask for his help. He was the key to everything.

Pyotr pushed his dish back with a grunt of appreciation. "Thanks for that," he said, and put his hand on top of mine on the table. "Roza, I've been thinking about you, I'm so sorry about Misha."

I shook my head and looked away. I believed that he was sorry. Pyotr feels things, Yulia, and he does care about me, just as I care about him. But I had no desire to go visit that black place inside me, when it could serve no useful purpose. But there was something that Pyotr might be able to help with—exposing the cruel way that females in the Red Army are treated.

"Pyotr, how would you like to do me a favor?" I began.

And I told him everything. About how my platoon has the worst quarters in the division, how the girls have to sleep with soldiers who have warmer beds just to survive. I told him about how Anya had been raped by General Kazarin, and how Masha had been forced to be an "army wife" during her first year at war, and how every girl in our platoon had been assaulted multiple times during her tour of duty, although most had been able to get away without being raped. I complained about how unfair it is that men can have as many partners as they want without anyone caring, while the female soldiers are called whores and prostitutes, both in the army and in civilian life, when most are actually quite modest girls who want to be left alone. I talked for a long time, and held nothing back.

Pyotr listened to me carefully, without interrupting. When I was done he had one question: "What's an army wife?"

"Basically, a sex slave," I said, "forced to live with an officer as his 'wife' so long as he wants her. Maybe she's taken from the local village where we're fighting, for an officer who likes the way a woman looks, or maybe she's a female soldier, like Masha, who has turned an officer's head, and is then reassigned to his command. The girl has no say in what happens to her."

Pyotr made a sound of disgust. "This is why the Germans and French have brothels at the frontlines. To avoid these kinds of troubles."

"They do?"

"Yes, they do. And I imagine the rest of the world does too. I can't think why the Red Army doesn't."

That was disturbing news, and I couldn't find any enthusiasm for the idea of a brothel at the frontlines, so I said nothing.

"So how did Masha escape from her officer?"

"He found someone else and let her go."

Pyotr shook his head. We regarded each other silently. "I have no words," he said finally.

"But Pyotr, words are exactly what you *do* have," I said.

"What do you mean?"

"You are the editor of an important newspaper," I said. "You have the power to get words out to people."

"Wait, so this is the favor? Oh no," he shook his head emphatically. "If I were to publish anything about this in *Destroy the Enemy*, I'd be thrown into prison faster than a Pole."

"Yes, I know," I said. "I wasn't thinking that you yourself would publish the article, but that you could send it out somewhere else to be published. Like maybe Canada?"

"It would never get past the censors."

"Isn't there some way?"

Pyotr snorted, looked wildly around the room, and leaned in close to me, knocking his mug over onto the white metal table.

"Roza," he said, in a low voice, "I'm uncomfortable even having this conversation. Do you know what a dangerous idea this is?"

"I'd be fine with you putting my name on the article," I said, righting his mug and using my sleeve to mop up the few drops of tea that had spilled.

He sat up straight and stared, looking at me like I had trout growing out of my ears.

"You can't be serious," he said.

"I'm dead serious."

"That's right, because you'd be *dead*."

I shrugged, sighed. "I'm going to die anyway, Pyotr. I want to do something good with my life. I always have. That's why I joined the army, to be useful, but it isn't working out the way I hoped it would. I can't be useful if they won't let me fight. So, here is another way!"

Pyotr didn't understand, but then, he's been mostly sheltered from combat. He hears about people dying, but doesn't see it happen, doesn't make it happen himself. He hasn't faced death in this war, and maybe he won't have to.

"Roza, you don't know that you'll be killed in combat!" he exclaimed.

I didn't know what to say to this, so I said nothing. How could I explain to him that somehow, I know I'm going to die on a battlefield?

"I'm not afraid to fight with the scouts," I said. "I've done it before and will do it again. I'm not afraid to die, Pyotr. Almost everyone I love has been killed. And I feel very strongly about this article. They've lied to us so often and for so long, not just about facts, or about what's real and what's a fake, but even about who we are. 'Look to our example of true equality between the sexes', they say, while they rape us and shelter us against our will! We aren't equal, what a joke! We don't even matter to them, except as sex objects."

"And you think men do matter to them?"

I paused in confusion. "Well no, all human life is cheap to the Party, but it's different, Pyotr. Men can do whatever they want to us girls. We are treated like possessions, without rights, like it used to be long ago. And this from the highest levels in the Red Army!"

"Shhh," Pyotr was looking around nervously, and I realized my voice had risen.

"And who is leader of the Red Army?" I whispered. "Stalin."

When I said his name out loud, I really thought Pyotr might have a stroke. He stood abruptly, the metal legs of his chair screeching against the concrete floor. "Let's walk," he said.

And so we walked, although it was very cold, along the Dnieper tributary that runs behind the rest home. The sun was strong overhead; its rays skittered across the surface of the frozen river in blinding jubilation. Beautiful. I sucked the sharp fresh air into my lungs and realized how much I missed being outdoors. Nature was a thousand times more intense than anything that could be found within the hospital.

"I'm worried about you, Roza," he said, and I laughed. *Poor Pyotr!*

"You might be the only one," I said.

"You think your mama doesn't care if you live or die?"

I stopped smiling at that. "I'm sure she cares."

"Sure she cares," he said, almost angrily. He stopped and faced me. "You are not alone, you know."

Oh yes I am, I thought. I said, "It's okay to be alone."

"Not if it means you get to ignore everyone who cares about you!"

"Who am I ignoring? I'm trying to be helpful, to do good, Pyotr! This isn't a selfish thing."

"You sure about that?"

"How is it selfish to put yourself at risk to expose a brutality, in hopes that something might get better for *other people*?"

He stopped walking and looked at me intently. "Don't you think it's selfish to die if you don't have to? That it will hurt the people who love you?"

I shook my head quickly—I knew my own mind here. "No, Pyotr. The people who really love me are already dead or soon will be, or have given me up for dead long ago. And in any case, isn't it more selfish to look the other way in order to stay alive?"

"So, I'm the selfish one in this scenario?"

I laughed. "Maybe. Depends on whether or not you help me." I winked at him.

He snorted and stuck his long nose into the air. We walked along in silence for a while, and he finally said, "Let me think about it. Figure out what's possible."

I knew he would help me, Yulia! This was the best possible response.

"No promises," he said sternly.

"No promises," I agreed. "But I know you'll do it."

As we made our way back to the rest home, I took the opportunity to tell him that both Sasha and Misha agreed with the philosophy of "believing what is good for you." Misha had his own way of looking the other way in order to stay alive. But that didn't work out so well for him, did it?

"I'm sorry you'll never be Roza Panarina," Pyotr said, as we parted. Brought tears to my eyes, Yulia.

But I'm excited about the possibility that we might be able to yank the veil off some of this nastiness in the Red Army, and maybe make a difference for *devotchkas* in the future. I hope!

1.Jan.45, 11:03
On the train to Arkhangelsk

It seems that while I'm not considered healed enough to go back to the war zone, the doctors agree that I don't need to lie in bed any longer. So, I've been given a week furlough, and am now sitting on the train to Arkhangelsk, waiting for it to leave the station. Hurrah! Something to do besides sleep, and stare at white walls. Naturally, it will be dark there most of the time now, and I'll be lucky if it's warmer than 10C, but I'm excited to go home.

3.Jan.45, 22:15
Naval base, Arkhangelsk

I got myself a room at the naval base for the week, as I didn't get any reply from my last letter to Anna Tamarova. I knocked on her door today, but no answer. Sad to think that she must have moved, and I have no way to get in touch with her. Maybe I'll never see my friend again.

It's not bad here, at the naval base, shelter from the cold and all that, but it's odd coming into the city from the direction of the White Sea. In all my years at Arkhangelsk, I've never slept on the sea side. Walking into town over the frozen harbor, I feel like a yeti or polar bear, or some warrior beast of the far north, returning to the city after an icy adventure. Everything seems foreign to me, and it doesn't help that I can't find any of my old friends. Perhaps they're all dead.

I remember Misha saying "We can never go home again, even if we survive this war." I thought he'd meant that we'd changed too much for things to be the same, because we'd killed people, because we'd seen war, because we'd moved on so far from where we came. But I see now that things at home have also moved on. Arkhangelsk is no longer my home. That's a hard thing to write, but it's true. Now I am truly a vagrant.

It seems a lifetime has passed, much more than two years, since I lived here, teaching at the Kindergarten #2. Still, I thought it would be the same. Silly. It was January of 1943 when I left Arkhangelsk for my *Vsevobuch* training. Six months later I went straight on to sniper school in Vishniaki, near Moscow. Near Misha's home. I would like to visit Misha's mother and sisters in Moscow, and give them his medal that I still carry in my rucksack. Maybe I'll get a chance to do that.

But today, it's Arkhangelsk. I spent the few hours of sunlight looking for old friends. Walked to the old school, in hopes of finding Anna Tamarova, but no luck. Went past the institute, with its frozen lake, and was content to see students out on the ice, hitting the bandy ball around. They were all girls, and I recognized no one, but they reminded me of my time at the institute, before the war, when we would spend Saturdays out on the ice, or watching the boys' bandy matches. That other lifetime.

If I'd had skates, I'd have gone out on the ice with the girls. Instead, I went for a coffee, read the paper, and saw that *Lermontov* was playing at the Ars Cinema. I have fond memories of the Ars, and decided to see the film. So glad that I did! Who hasn't read *Death of a Poet*, and *Hero of our Time*? But without knowing much about him as a person, I connected to his character from the moment the movie started, all the way through until the end. I saw myself in him, strongly. He spent his life ignoring what people told him to do, and chose his own path. The image of him standing alone on an iron bridge — I'll never forget it. So powerful! Yes, he was alone, but that was his choice, that was how he stayed true to his character. I will follow his example, and live as if I were truly alone, because who needs family and friends, when everyone dies in the end? And before they die, they often betray. It's in the human character. You know I could never mean you, Yulia.

After the film ended, as I was headed back to base, I found myself walking next to a little boy who was on his own, wandering slowly up the street.

"*Privet*,"[49] I said. He ignored me and continued dragging his stick against a fence.

"Shouldn't you be getting home? It's very cold tonight."

"Don't have a home," he shrugged.

This took me by surprise, in one so little. Street orphans are common, as we know, Yulia, but usually they run together in bands, I've never seen such a young boy on his own.

"What's your name?"

"Misha," he said, and I smiled. A common enough name.

"And your surname?"

He stopped and looked up at me. "Kasantsev. I am called Misha Kasantsev."

"And how old are you, Misha?"

"Four," he said, carefully holding up four fingers.

"Don't you have a mama or a papa?"

"No, but I have an aunt," he said solemnly, "and she is very mean."

"Oh," I hid my smile. "I'm so sorry."

"Can I kiss you?" he blurted out. "I have never kissed a girl, and you are very pretty, and I would like to."

I laughed. "Sure, give me a kiss," I said, and squatted down to his level.

He kissed me on both cheeks, wet and sloppy kisses, but he was so sweet and innocent, and I had to fight to not cry.

---

49 *Privet*—Russian for "hello."

"Thank you, Misha," I said. "You are the best thing to happen to me today."

He grinned up at me.

"And I think you should go home to your aunt, even though she is mean. It will get very cold tonight, and it's important to have a warm place to sleep."

"She will beat me for being outside after dark," he mumbled, looking down again.

I nodded, felt sorry for him. "Best to get it over with," I said. "But first, give me one more kiss." I presented my cheek to him, and he threw his arms around my neck. I hugged him back, hard.

"Don't forget," I whispered in his ear, "that there are lots of people in the world who aren't mean."

We let go and looked at each other. I took off my new blue scarf and wrapped it around his neck.

Never take off your scarf, came Mama's fierce whisper, as it had every time I'd removed a scarf since I was eight years old. I think in this case, she would not have minded so much.

"Take this scarf to your aunt, as a gift, from Roza Shanina. Maybe she will be kinder. Go home now. Do you promise?"

He nodded earnestly and ran off. I watched him disappear down the street, wondering what would become of him. Will his life be built around war and famine? Will he grow to beat his own children? Maybe he will escape his fate, and go to Switzerland, or America. Unlikely.

I turned back toward the base, walking alone in the cold darkness, but I was not afraid to be out by myself in Arkhangelsk, as I sometimes have been. I think I prefer it this way. There is peace in solitude, and I am enough, with the occasional kindness of strangers, even the very young ones.

4.Jan.45, 19:47
Naval base, Arkhangelsk

Missing Mama tonight, who raised three orphans out of the goodness of her heart, along with the seven of us kids. She has a kind heart, and in many ways she was a good mother, although I wish she had taken my side even once with Papa. When he slapped me, she would busy herself, humming, always looking away. I wonder, what was her truth in those moments?

Such a soft woman, our mother, and yet it was so unkind to let Papa treat us like wayward cows who needed to be dogged back into the lee. I love her, truly I do. She hasn't yet slipped through the holes in my heart. But I don't understand how she has put up with him for all these years, and I can't forgive her for being willing to lose me, her daughter, to basically give me up for dead, to appease Papa. How could she do that? How could she let him beat me and kick me out of the house at fourteen years old, while stroking the hair of the three-year-old orphan child she had taken in?

I would never behave so, and when a man tries to hit me, I fight back with everything I have. But she isn't a fighter, and maybe that's where the trouble comes in. He is so much stronger than she, physically, mentally. She could never win.

I understand that she's afraid of him. Intimidation is the best tool of men like my papa. The body has a primitive reaction to fear. The heart pounds, the blood rushes to your head, muddies your thoughts. Fear can paralyze you, so that you cannot think, you cannot function. Papa knows this well, and he wields fear like a weapon, as a means of controlling Mama and everyone else. He's very good at it. *The ends justify the means*, he'd say. He controlled Sergei, and tried to do the same with me, with all of us, but especially me, because I fought against him and did as I pleased, whatever he thought about it. Fear didn't keep me in line the way it did with the others, because for me it turned into anger. Papa hated that he could not control me, and I hated him for trying.

And look at Sergei now, in prison, as a result of letting Papa control his life. Not that Sergei was so innocent, but he was weak. I don't know who the real Sergei is. He always went along with Papa, perhaps believing that Papa's legacy would become his own. In some ways, Sergei got the worst of it.

When I was twelve, I figured out that the fear of getting beaten is worse than the strike of the fist itself. Pain is predictable, but fear—fear takes our lives out of our own hands. The first time I pushed back against the fear, yanked myself out of the paralysis, it took tremendous effort, like punching a fist out of my soul from a place of total stillness. It's much easier now. If I ever see my mother again, I'll teach her how to do this.

Mama never took my part with Papa because she was frozen with fear. I see this with my head, I accept it, but my heart can't forgive her. She sacrificed me, her daughter, to this great weakness of hers. I can't help but wonder what horrible thing could have happened if she'd brought herself to look clearly at the not-infrequent brutality and cruelty of her husband. Would she have been unable to carry on? Would it have made her less kind, less herself? What was she protecting? Not me. Maybe she was just weak. I wish I knew what she achieved by sacrificing me. Did the ends justify the means?

When I left home at fourteen, after that horrible fight, I thought *the hell with you both*. I was certain that anything would be better than living at home, and in the end, it worked out pretty well. My life hasn't been easy, but I've done things on my own terms, and that brings me a feeling of satisfaction. But I miss my mama.

8.Jan.45, 20:36
184th RD

Got back to the rest home yesterday to get checked out by the doctor, and he released me back to the Front. Hurrah! My shoulder is much better, hardly even stiff this morning. I went straight from the hospital to Smolensk headquarters and sought out General Ponomarev, who is a big brass member of the council, in hopes that he would assist me in getting deployed to the Front, rather than back to my platoon. The girls have been fine without me, so it seems like the perfect time to transfer to a forward company. Ponomarev saw me, but was very busy and clearly did not want to deal with my request. He sent me to General Krylov, commander of the Fifth Army.

When I walked into Krylov's office, his eyes swept me up and down and he frowned. I wasn't sure what was lacking, but I felt ashamed. It may have been my uniform, which was not in the greatest shape, the shoulder torn and bloodied, but I hadn't had a chance to swap it out for a new one.

"Thank you for seeing me, comrade General," I said.

"You're Roza Shanina?"

"Yes sir, Senior Sergeant Roza Shanina, commander of the sniper platoon in the 184th Rifle Division."

He peered at me curiously from his great swivel chair.

"Take a seat," he said, gesturing to some small metal chairs that were huddled together, facing his desk.

I chose the closest chair and sat, which put me several inches below the General. He looked down at me from his high and roomy swivel chair, and I thought of a huge bronze statue of the Buddha that I had once seen in a Moscow museum.

"Naturally I know who you are, from the newspapers," he said, grabbing a walnut from a bowl on his desk and cracking it open.

"You seem to be doing a fine job for the People's Army." He threw the nut meat into his mouth and chewed noisily. "What can I do for you, Sergeant Shanina?"

"Thank you, comrade General. Thank you for that. I hope I'm a good soldier, but I don't get as much combat time as I'd like."

He cracked open another walnut and continued to chew, occasionally glancing at me. He didn't seem likely to comment, so I went on.

"I would like to be transferred to a company that conducts offensive attacks, rather than defensive ones," I said. Might as well get right to it.

"Snipers are useful in defensive positions," he said. "Support against counter-attacks, securing the area, recon, that sort of thing."

"*Da*, but would not a sniper be just as useful in an offensive action?"

He brushed some walnut debris from his chest and folded his hands on his desk, giving me his full attention. He no longer reminded me of the Buddha at all.

"Well, for one thing," he said, "offensive units are always on the move. They need to be ready to push into enemy territory at every moment. Snipers sit still and wait for their targets to come to them."

"That's true, comrade General, but I myself am known for being accurate at speed. I hold the record for doublets at the Women's Central Sniper School."

"Sniper school! This isn't a classroom, young lady."

I flustered at that. Good job, Roza, bring up your school marks to the commander of the Fifth Army!

"Sergeant Shanina, the Red Army has a policy to protect women snipers from harm, when possible. You do realize that your chances of surviving the war will go down a lot if you fight with an offensive unit? I can't see any good reason to send the Soviet Union's darling sniper to her death."

There it was again—proof that they wanted to keep me around to put my picture on the front of their newspapers.

"Comrade General, if I were a boy, would you grant my request for a transfer?" I asked, crisply.

"Are you going to surprise me by turning out to be a boy?"

A nervous laugh escaped me. "No! But if I were a boy making this request, would it be granted?"

He waggled his head back and forth, and said "I don't know. These things are handled lower down in the ranks, and every case is different."

"*Khorosho*,[50] what about the last male soldier who asked for a transfer to the Front. Was his request granted?"

"I have no idea, Roza."

"Sergeant Shanina."

"What?" he looked at me in surprise.

"Beg your pardon, comrade General, but it's Senior Sergeant Shanina."

He let out a loud bark of laughter. "Fiesty, aren't you?"

"I've been called worse," I shrugged, and leaned in. "Comrade General, you have before you a commanding officer, thrice decorated by the Red Army, who is asking permission to fight for the Motherland. How can you not allow it?"

"Comrade Sergeant, you *are* fighting for the Motherland, as a sniper, doing exactly what snipers do, which is to support special operations and provide defense for counter-attacks," he said. "And we appreciate your service."

"But the action at the rear is nothing," I cried, losing my cool. "You yourself must know that the German army is retreating, that the defensive opportunities get thinner each moment!"

"I'm not inclined to allow it," he said, shaking his head.

---

50 *Khorosho*—Russian expression meaning something like "okay" or "very well."

Don't cry, don't cry. I willed myself to stay calm. "Comrade General, if you only knew how much I want to be at the frontlines. It's the only thing left for me. There's nothing else. I've proven myself in battle, over and over. Why does the life of one soldier matter so much anyway? I can be helpful to the cause at the Front."

I heard myself pleading, and was ashamed, but I couldn't stop. The monster in my chest demanded to be appeased. I had to go to the Front, and here was the man who had the power to make that happen.

He watched me for a moment, his brow scrunched up.

"Comrade General, please."

He appeared to be thinking for another minute, and then bounced his palms on his desk with a loud slap. "All right, comrade Shanina. You can go to the frontlines with the new offensive that starts on the fifth of February."

"The fifth of February!" I exclaimed. That was a lifetime away, and I was ready to leave immediately.

"*Da*, the fifth of February," he said loudly. "Any problem with that?"

"No, no problem. Thank you, comrade General." I didn't want to seem ungrateful.

"You'll get the authorization papers before the offensive begins."

"Thank you." I wanted to say more, to think of something that would allow me to go forward straight away.

"You can go now, comrade Shanina," Krylov said, looking pointedly at the door.

I got up to leave, wondering how on earth I was going to get through the next few weeks at the rear of the division.

On the way back to my platoon, I stopped by the girls' divisional headquarters to get a new uniform. Luck was with me and I scored a sniper's fur coat, a *telogreika*,[51] new boots, and new winter camouflage. Plus, they gave me my own Willys with a driver to take me around. I thought *Roza Shanina is moving up in the world!* But in reality, it was freezing cold, driving around in the open-air jeep.

I was eager to shoot my rifle, and had my driver take me directly to the trench where my platoon was working, on the border of Lithuania and Belarus, and I jumped from the freezing jeep into the freezing trench. The girls seemed pleased to see me, but there was no action for *Zhanna*.

We're back at our bunker now, and the mood is changed, more somber than before. Five girls had been killed while I was gone, including my friend Tanya Karevna, who was a very good and interesting sort of girl. No more Tani! So sad. And then I noticed that Sasha Ekimova's things were gone. What happened to Sasha? It turns out that she and Vovka got married two weeks ago, and she has moved into his bunker.

I'm low, Yulia. Very sad to hear about Tanya and the others, and sorry to lose Sasha. We'll still see her, naturally, but everything will be different. The Stray Troika is split up. Vovka is Sasha's family now, and Kali and I will have to share quarters with others. Kaleriya Petrova and I have never tried to be friends with just the two of us — Sasha has always been there.

Marriage and death, the two biggest pieces of news, and somehow they both feel like death. Kali tells me that Sasha has blossomed, that she's happy, and I'm glad for her, truly. She finally has what she has long wanted — a legitimate place with her Vovka, and the warm bed that goes with it. But the platoon no longer feels like home, with Sasha gone.

After supper, I went with some of the girls to the 157th and didn't like it at all. It was like walking into a den of hungry wolves; the

---

51 *Telogreika* — a warm, wool-padded jacket, Russian for "body warmer."

men were on the prowl and their comrade Major was the big tiger predator. Shortly after we got there, I learned that some of the girls had been raped recently, very easily, like before, and I refused to stay the night. I walked back to our freezing bunker and will sleep in the cold tonight.

It's been a sad homecoming for me, Yulia, and I see that I don't belong here. It doesn't feel like home anymore.

You can never go home, Misha said, and this is so true, Yulia. We can only go forward—those of us who still can.

10.Jan.45

It's freezing cold in our bunker—I think I would be warmer if I were lying naked in the snow. It's hard to manage, even for a northerner like me. I dread going to bed. Last night, it was so cold that I was forced to get up and leave the bunker in the middle of the night, in search of a warmer spot. I ended up staying with a major in his bunker. We kissed and it was nice, but before long, it went further. I tell myself lies.

I feel bad, sick. No sleep last night and today we were bombarded by Germans all morning long, until the *Katyushas* arrived and peppered the Fritz. Our trench was right under the line of fire, and my God, the shriek of those rockets! I'd forgotten what it's like to hear them over your head, the constant human-like wails rushing toward us as the rockets flew over our heads, then dying off as they zoomed in on the enemy. Over and over again, for hours, we sat in the smoke-filled trench and covered our ears to the sound of the rockets. So funny to think about how worried we were last spring to have the guns shooting over our heads. It's nothing now—a fly in our tea.

It's late afternoon, and we have orders to move forward. I'm waiting for the girls to finish packing up and we will be gone. My ears ring, my lungs rasp and my brain has scurried off somewhere to hide. But I'll lead the platoon forward, marching in frozen boots, because nothing less would be expected of a Soviet soldier.

I'm sorry for my foul mood, Yulia. Maybe tomorrow will be better.

12 January 1945

We are now on the Belarus side of the border, sitting in the snow. Our right flank finally took Pillkallen yesterday, and now they are paused, waiting for the signal to go forward. Our left flank has gone already, they must be deep in German territory by now, while we sit and listen to distant gunfire and the thunder of cannons. There are no more horses and no trucks for us, so we carry all of our possessions on our backs. All morning long we've been waiting, ready to march.

I think they've forgotten us entirely, and who could blame them? We are not important to the offensive effort. We'll never get the signal to go forward. My feet are itchy from being frozen and needing to move, but we'll never leave supply, we will die here in the snow, from cold or starvation, I know it. No dinner last night and no breakfast this morning. What can we do but sleep in the snow dreaming of dead comrades and ignoring the pain in our stomachs?

I don't mean to complain, Yulia, I hate when people complain, but why stay here, where nothing is happening, where I'm not needed? The restlessness will kill me before the lack of food or a stray bullet. If I'm going to be starved out in the cold, why not be cold and hungry at the Front, where interesting things are happening, where there's a chance for me to be useful? Where there's a chance — dear God! — to feel like myself again.

15.Jan.1945, 8:00
Still on the border of Belarus and Lithuania

The girls are all going to the bath, as there's nothing else to do, but I'm leaving. It's a certain thing — there's nothing for me here but frustration and memories of how things used to be. Kali has agreed to cover for me, and will wait two days after I've gone before she reports that I've been injured and have gone to the field hospital. My last good friend! I'll miss Kali. Maybe we'll meet again one day.

I've put on my white camouflage, kissed everyone goodbye, even the girls who were mean to me, as I don't care enough to hold a grudge, and arranged for a ride in a Willys with two of the communications guys. In one hour I should be at the Front, which this morning moved twenty kilometers toward Königsberg.

Waiting now for the driver, and I wonder what does the future hold for me? Will this be the last unrevokable charge, or the start of something new? Maybe both. I'm ready for it, whatever happens.

16.Jan.45, midnight
Well into Belarus, in the thick of the frontline camps

Spent last night in the 144th with General Donets and was well received by everyone. Friendly guys. Donets told me to report to

Commander General Kasimov for proper orders, and I went first thing this morning, but I wasn't admitted to see him, and his lieutenant didn't know who I was.

"I am reporting for duty as ordered by comrade Donets," I told him, but he wouldn't let me in.

"You have no papers," the lieutenant said pointedly, "and the Commander General is a very busy man. I can't let you in."

No attempt to appeal to him gained the slightest measure of success, and eventually he became angry and shouted at me to leave. How funny that the one time it might have been useful to be recognized, my fate was in the hands of this character, who apparently never reads a newspaper.

It would've been easier if I'd been accepted into a unit with real orders, especially in this cold weather, and without having eaten much in days, but I gave the idea up as a dead duck. Like Lermontov, I will make my own way.

My dead captain's watch tells me it's midnight. I have a small fire, and my *plash palatka*. If I bury myself in the snow, I should make it through the night. And as long as I'm writing to you, I'll never be completely alone, but I can't stop crying. Who do I need? What do I need, and what am I good for? I have no food, no friends, and nowhere to be. No papers, no authorization, no battles. I'm constantly under fire, but have nowhere to point *Zhanna*. Everything is different now — it is chaos, a dark, animal chaos, with the blizzard adding to the frenzy of it. Today, I watched some of our guys shoot seven German children, the youngest barely walking and the older ones ten or eleven. Just a few years younger than you, Yulia. Then they dragged the frau of the village off into the woods on a tractor. We have permission now to kill all Germans, to do whatever we please, not just the soldiers. It's so ugly, Yulia. I know how the *fashisty* behaved during Barbarossa, I know about their "scorched earth" policy. I've heard about the Nazi death camps, where Anya and

Lyuba are likely detained, if they're even alive. They are monsters, yes. But Yulia, in our country, it's not the monsters who fight, but the everyday, good people. Maybe they're the same as us. Monsters tell us what to do, and then we kill each other. I'm not easy about killing civilians, especially children, and I can't even think about how our guys treat the frau. A disease has come over these men, who are otherwise good, everyday people. Now they blend together into a dark beast that wants to cause as much pain as possible, and it's allowed, even encouraged. Where is the humanity? I can't bear it.

The boys don't want the *devotchkas* to know what they do to the frau of the villages. They say they milk chickens, but we know what that means. At least they have the decency to be ashamed of themselves.

And while this darkness grows all around me, I can only watch, without even shooting my rifle. There are no battles for me.

"We have enough support troops. Go back to your platoon."

But I can't go back. By now, Kali will have reported that I was injured, so they won't expect me at the platoon. And I would prefer to be here, in all its horror, with bullets whistling past, because I feel dead at the rear. Here, at least I know I'm alive. Everywhere else I'm just waiting, sleeping, until I can come back to life on the Front. I need the bullets and chaos, the danger and challenge. Without the challenge of battle, I'm the living dead.

But what to do next? I'm weak. I need food, and sleep. And some good cheer, some friends, a loving caress. But that's too much to hope for. Somehow, I've lost Lida's cross, and my heart wants to break for this. I reached into my pocket this afternoon and found only a small hole—no gold cross. No chance of finding it in this blizzard. Why didn't I send it back to her family with her other things? What made me think I had the right to keep it for myself? Selfish, just like with Misha's medal that I have stowed in my rucksack. And now Lida's cross is lost forever, like everything that was once important to me.

All around me are the warm bunkers and trenches of rifle companies, but I'm not welcome, except as a guest in some officer's bed, and I'm not willing to go there. I'm a war hero, with two Orders of Glory and an Order of Courage, and I cannot rest my head with my army, or get a bite to eat, or even a job to do. I know that I'm a good soldier, willing to put myself in harm's way, showered with glory in the papers, but no one wants me. What was the point of joining the army? One more year at the institute and I'd have qualified for university.

Ours is not to reason why, ours is but to do or die.

Da, Misha. But this life is so hard, so demanding, and my heart is shredded to pieces. I don't love anyone now. What would be the point? Love is not an asset out here. Why make friends when everyone dies?

I want only to be useful. That's all that is left to me, and since the monster won't let me be anywhere but here, I will be here, doing sniper work. That's my real strength, that's how I can be useful. If they would only give me a combat job! It's the only thing I crave.

Yulia, I hope that you'll have the life we used to dream about. If that wish comes true, then all of this loss and desperation, it will have been worth it. I hope you will go to university, and study something serious, and if you want, leave the *kolkhoz*. I see now that it isn't so bad, our village in the *taiga*, but rather beautiful, with its simplicity and insufficiencies. But don't become Mama, with her hands destroyed by milking cows all day every day, and the rest of her time spent turning the other cheek. Get married, by all means, but only to a man you can truly love. Have children, because I know you would like that, and would be a sweet mother. And be brave, Yulia, because fear causes all kinds of evil, and there is nothing so bad that it's worth fearing. Be yourself, and do what you want, but please live a long, rich life, for me, and that will make it all worthwhile. I can sit by a pitiful fire in this dark, frozen land, starving, asking only for one more battle, if I know that you will be safer because of my sacrifices.

If I survive the night, I'll try again tomorrow.

17.Jan.45

Slept badly, buried under the snow and dirt. Lida Vdovina's dead eyes visited me again and again, reproaching me for losing her cross. At least I knew where I was the instant I woke up. This howling blizzard brought me to my senses right away. Or maybe I was never truly asleep.

Where will I find my next battle? I will not be easy until I figure this out. There are lots of companies out here, surely one of them will take in a good soldier, who has nothing to prove and nothing to lose. I can bounce around until I find a place to belong. God knows I've done it before.

Still shocked by how different this place is, compared to the war I've known until now. It's not at all like the frontlines in Lithuania. We're very close to Germany now, and the sun has been shrouded by a great blizzard, making everything black and scary—the perfect setting for a scene of human desperation. There are no rainbow sparkles on the snow, no bright spots on the horizon. I think all the goodness in the land has fled, knowing that something terrible is happening. What remains? A lot of grey shapes that blend into a curtain of dark holes, a stage prop for the war theater. The storm blows up snow and grey dirt into the air, pummeling everything. I stand out in my white camouflage, and that's dangerous. I would be easy to target. And it's true that I don't know this place, that I don't belong. It doesn't feel real to me. But I have faith that the sun will continue to rise as it always has, behind the giant storm cloud.

There is nothing new under the sun, Mama says.

Da, Mama, this has all happened before. This is the way of it. Death, who has the power to level all living things, means nothing to the sun; it will continue to rise and set on the earth, while those who have been killed in action get mixed back into the soil, and feed the turnips, or carrots, or onions. I'd rather not be an onion.

God, I need to shake this dark spirit. *After a storm, fair weather. After sorrow, joy.* I'll try to get with the gunners of the 216th tomorrow. Good, down-to-earth guys, they always like me, and are always going to battle. I can act as support for the guys on the turrets. It's a dangerous job, right on the Front—that's the job for me. I only wonder if I should ask permission, or just go.

19.Jan.45, 19:50
Alone again, by my small fire

The snow has slowed down, which is good for the fire, but I miss the insulation on top of my *plash palatka*. I'm tired, right down to my bones. My body is tired, my mind is tired. I'm exhausted with my life.

You and I were raised with a lot of talk about equality between the sexes, unlike Mama and Papa, who grew up under the Tsar. Some of this talk may be true, like equal conditions for factory workers and such. I didn't think about this much growing up, always thinking I would do whatever I wanted, whether I was a girl or a boy. Maybe it was the same for you. But in this life, at war, I've been forced to look at it. In the Red Army, females are thought inferior, and sometimes treated as prey, rather than comrades. Whatever anyone says, this is the truth of it. I've seen it again and again, and although I don't like to tell you some of the things that happen to me, because they are ugly, unpleasant, not serene, I know that I can't stop you from growing up, and you may as well know the worst of it. I had trouble with a man last night, and only escaped because I'm strong, or at least, was strong enough to fight him off. This was not the first attempt of its kind, but it was the worst. I'm rattled.

Yesterday, early in the morning, I went to the 216th rifle division to join up with them. Rather than report for duty in the official way, I went to the field kitchen to see who I could meet and try for some breakfast, and guess who I saw? Captain Pavel Blokhin, by the porridge.

"Roza Shanina!" he said, with a smile. "How are you here?"

I was greatly surprised by this greeting, so much friendlier than any I'd had from him in the past. I greeted him warily and kept my eyes on the *kasha* the cook was spooning into my bowl.

"Are you working in this company now?"

I paused to take a bite of the porridge and felt immediate comfort as it slid down my throat into my stomach, warming my insides. So good. "Is there anything better than *kasha*?"

He looked at me more closely. "You're really hungry, aren't you? Sit, eat, we'll talk later."

And he took care of me, Pavel Blokhin. Got me another bowl of *kasha* and even some NZ rations to put in my pack. Why the change, I wanted to know, but he just shrugged, saying I wasn't his responsibility anymore. He didn't even ask to see my papers, Yulia! And he introduced me to the tankers, who invited me to go to battle with them that same day in a T-34. I agreed, with the idea that I would work as a loader.

This was my first time inside a tank during battle, and I was excited as I climbed aboard, but the reality of the tank was pretty bad. The smoke was horrible! My eyes burned so much that they were useless, and I could barely breathe. It's just that I'm not used to it, I think, but I ended up with a terrible headache and a sick stomach. Worse, I was a useless piece of baggage on their mission, too sick to do anything but suffer in silence.

At some point while the tank was crashing through barriers, with me trying to keep my breakfast down, one of the other tanks was hit, and the guys inside were shredded up. An old friend of Sasha's, comrade Major Tubanov, was killed. But the mission was successful despite my uselessness—we cleared the area east of the village.

I learned one thing from the tankers—I can't work in a tank, sitting for hours in an ice box full of diesel smoke. When I crawled out of the damned thing this afternoon, my head throbbed so badly I would have cheerfully chopped it off. All I wanted was to lie down, but where to go? I'm homeless now, on the Front, with no orders, and no one expecting me.

Then I saw Blokhin, talking to a guy I didn't know, waving me over. I stumbled toward him, almost blind with pain.

"Like the tanks?" he asked, and I could hear the smirk in his voice.

I thought I might collapse if I didn't find a place to lie down soon, and asked Blokhin to point me in the direction on the female quarters.

"There aren't any, far as I know," he replied, "but you're welcome in my bed."

Can you believe, Yulia, that I was so ill that I let that comment slide past without taking its meaning? I let him take me by the arm and lead me to his bunker, which was toasty warm and bathed in an orange glow. I'd been cold for so long that I nearly cried when I stepped in. It was almost as good as a hot bath.

"Thank you, comrade Captain," I sighed. "I'll just curl up on the floor and stay out of your way."

But he had to go out, and said he didn't need his bed for now, so I could use it if I chose. My body was done for the day, for many days if given its choice, and I sat heavily on the bunk, grabbing my head to hold still the pain that was slicing into my eyeballs.

"Have a rest, and I'll see you later," Blokhin said.

He may have been speaking normally or even quietly, but to me he seemed to be shouting, every word stabbed into my temples. With great effort, I opened my eyes to look at him, and got distracted by my own face taped to the wall behind him. A newspaper cutting.

Strange, seeing my photo on the wall, and with the headache and the exhaustion, I got confused. "Is that me?"

"*Da*. Been seeing you a lot in the papers lately. This one's my favorite," he said, then he sat next to me on the bed and lowered his voice. "Not as good as the real thing."

I looked at him and was overcome with nausea. I bolted up and just made it outside the bunker before my stomach revolted and I vomited all over his entryway. "Sorry," I groaned.

He waved that off. "You'll feel better if you take some vodka," he said, and fetched a bottle and glasses from under his bunk.

"No, I wouldn't," I said, and felt I might vomit again at the idea.

Blokhin paused, bottle in hand. "No drink?" he asked, eyebrows knit together. Then he shrugged and poured one for himself and tossed it down his throat. Then he left, and I laid down and fell asleep instantly.

Sometime later, I woke up when someone crawled into bed with me, and here's where the trouble began. I tensed the instant his body hit the bed, reaching for *Zhanna*, but she was not lying next to me like she usually is—I'd left her resting against the wall five feet away. If she'd been handy, I might have used her on this intruder.

"Easy, soldier," the man slurred, and I breathed in a noseful of vodka. I recognized Blokhin's voice, and also realized that my headache was gone. My whole body sighed with relief. This was not an enemy attack, it was Captain Pavel Blokhin, who I knew well, coming to sleep in his own bed.

I sat up, thinking to give him back his bed, but he wrapped a meaty arm around me and pulled me into him, sliding his left arm under my waist.

"So nice to find you warming my bed," he said, and began kissing my neck and grabbing at my breasts over the top of my *telnyashka*.

"*Stoy*," I said, pushing his hands away.

But he didn't stop, Yulia. He thrust himself into my behind and started to pull at my pants, and I came fully awake and elbowed him, hard.

He cried out in pain and clutched his side, and I froze, terrified, wondering if I had just attacked a commanding officer. It was self-defense, truly. What else could I do?

Maybe he thought I was an army whore, that I'd go along with it. Maybe that's what other girls do in these situations, with an officer who has the power to do as he pleases.

My paralysis lasted long enough for him to roll on top of me and pin me down. He held my jaw and neck with one hand and grabbed the waist of my pants with the other, trying to rip them off, and I no longer wondered about the right way to behave.

"Get OFF!" I yelled, struggling against him, but he was so big! It was like pushing against rock. He increased the pressure of his thumb on my neck, and my vision started to go white. In a flash of adrenalin and muscle memory, I yanked my knee up into his groin, and felt a rush of victory when his thumb slipped off my neck. I shoved him with the strength of my anger, and watched in surprise as he rolled off the bed and landed on the floor with a loud thud, curled in pain.

I scrambled up and stood over him, fixing my pants and fighting the urge to kick him.

"*Blyat*,"[52] he snarled.

At that, I pulled my dagger from my leg wrappings and flashed it close to his face. "Pavel Blokhin, you will not touch me."

"You gonna kill me?" he asked, his face red and ugly with anger. "Great headline. 'Roza Shanina slays Hero of the Soviet Union in his bed.'"

"Don't tempt me," I said coldly, and he spat at me, but only landed a little spittle on my pants, because I had the upper position. I laughed, towering over him, reveling in my power, however briefly held.

"Get out," he rasped.

"*Yes sir*, comrade Captain," I said, and yanked my boots on. My heart was pounding in my ears, and I was afraid I'd face trouble for this. I grabbed my rifle and rucksack.

"You're nothing, Roza Shanina. I've had *frau* better than you."

I paused to look at this man, this vile creature. So he was one of *them*, one of the soldiers who raped and killed the German frau, in exactly the same way the *Eizengruppen* had raped and killed our people at the beginning of the war.

Last thing I heard before slamming the bunker door was—"You're gonna regret this, fucking *zenschina*."

To hell with him. My God. How had I ever thought I'd be in safe hands with this man? What would have happened if he wasn't sloppy with vodka, or if I was still down with a headache?

My legs shook as I fled, fast as I could, and I could hardly breathe for crying. I ran into the woods and walked for a long while, maybe fifteen kilometers along the Front, and cried the whole time, all the way from my heart. Why did things that mattered in the outside

---

52 *Blyat*—Russian for "bitch whore."

world have no meaning in our life at war? Why did we treat each other so badly? Does love even exist in the war zone? Or friendship, or basic respect? Yes, we could all be killed at any time. Shouldn't that make us kinder, rather than the opposite?

I missed Misha so badly in that moment — it was a physical pain. I wouldn't be here, wandering the frontlines, if Misha were alive — I'd be with him. But it's better that he doesn't know how Blokhin behaved, that he didn't feel a need to avenge me, because that could never happen. There's no justice here, only power, and human life is cheap.

I was so alone, bullets whistling past, fires burning in the distance. With no one there to witness my sobbing, I let the feelings pour out of me. Misha's death, Blokhin's betrayal. My own betrayal of myself for misjudging Blokhin and putting myself in a bad position. I wandered through the woods, paying no attention to where I was going, until I heard German voices, and retraced my footsteps as quickly as possible until I was within earshot of our camp.

Crying again, as I write by my lonely little fire. So tired of crying — let's add that to the list of things I'm sick of. It's a weakness in me. I've never felt so weak as I do now, but somehow, I belong here, although I'm homeless. Although it's all become so ugly. I can't be anywhere else.

I miss Sasha and Kali, my sisters-in-arms. But that's in the past, and I must go forward, alone. Lermontov wanted to be alone, it was his greatest desire, and maybe it's better. I'm not afraid of it, but how much easier to have a job! And orders, food, a warm place to sleep.

I can only keep trying, and eventually I'll make my way into a unit and get more battle time. It's the only way. Tomorrow, I'll ask for a job with the 157th.

I hope your bed is warm, my Yulia, and your store of potatoes vast. And Mama and Papa and Marat, and the orphans — I hope everyone is well. I don't blame Papa anymore for what happened.

I know that I have a share of the guilt. Tell him for me, if I don't get the chance.

21.Jan.45, 23:50

I entered the 157th yesterday, easily, and with orders. They hired me to defend the supply truck drivers, and ride in the cabs. An easy job, warm, and I got to eat with the guys. There isn't much food anywhere, everything is thin, so I take what I can get and don't complain. The Third Front has moved ten kilometers in the past three days, and the Second has gone sixty in the same time. We're really on our way to Germany now, making progress, but with many casualties.

Yesterday was good, riding in the cabs, being warm, with food to eat, but I decided not to stay with the cargo guys. The monster in my chest was eager to push me forward, toward the thick of the action, and I couldn't resist. ("Oh passion, passion, oh blind strivings of the human heart! Onward, onward, it sayeth, and where beauty leads, there it follows." —Theodore Dreiser, *Sister Carrie*) I left this morning, with the infantry of the 157th, to head to the frontlines. But through some error, we moved forward without reporting to the rear, and our own *Katyushas* and fiddlers hit us. God and Hell, we were ground up! Body parts everywhere. This was the first time I've been on the target side of the *Katyushas*, and now I understand why the Germans are so afraid of them. We lost many to "friendly fire" before the rocket boys learned who we were. Then we could only bandage the wounded, say goodbye to the dead, and move forward.

The objective was another big house, and we rushed it in three groups, I on the northern side. We took the house easily, but it changed our division because we were split apart during the rush forward. I ended up with the 371st RD inside the house, and could not go further, with Fritz shelling us with all sorts of weapons: self-propelled guns, machine guns, shells. They had a store of weapons about a hundred meters behind the house, in a ravine, and they shot at us constantly. I positioned myself in a window on the house's upper floor and shot at the Fritz working the guns. Got one sure kill when a head popped out of a hatch, otherwise not sure how many kills from the house. It was too far to see into the shadows.

Found a thick, empty book of paper in the house, and took it gratefully. My next journal! When I went down to the kitchen, the guys threw filthy compliments at me. There's filthy language everywhere—the worst I've ever experienced. There seems to be an unspoken rule in effect that nothing can be said unless it is spoken in the most offensive way humanly possible. I won't repeat these things to you, Yulia.

I left the house and went off on my own, retreating back toward the command post, where I got some food and stumbled across some acquaintances. I learned from them that only six are alive in the company I fought with today. This morning, we were seventy-eight. I also learned that Pavel Blokhin was killed yesterday. My first reaction? *Good, he got what he deserved*, and then, *Yay, I will not be punished*. Shame came next, quickly, like ice dumped on my head. I cried as I left command post, mostly from frustration, from not knowing how to think or feel. And perhaps I am to blame, partially. He went into battle with no sleep, probably still drunk, and he was killed. If I hadn't been there, where I wasn't supposed to be, would Captain Pavel Blokhin still be alive? Maybe, but I don't know, Yulia. I take myself too seriously.

Sometimes I think—what good am I, after all? Blokhin wasn't a good guy, but he was a hero, five times decorated, now dead. Maybe I should have just shared his bed? Who I am I to think I'm more important than he? But no, I couldn't, not like that. Everything inside me resists.

Do I still hold fast to the laws? "The law makes a crawling snail of one who would soar in eagle's flight." That's right. I want to fly, not crawl! To be an extraordinary warrior.

Again, I'm showered with glory. I picked up Malchonov's recent paper, in which he wrote: "Distinguished Shanina was award the medal 'For Courage' for actions during an enemy counter-attack. An honorable sniper in our units." And the December *Spark* journal, out of Moscow, which featured my image on the cover, and said that I had killed 54 Germans and taken three prisoners. I wonder if the entire Soviet Union has seen this. You must have seen it, Yulia, along with the whole family. My heart is full for what you must have felt, seeing my picture and reading about my achievements. But a niggling part of me still sneers at me, saying it's not real. I try hard to be good, and I guess I'm a good sniper, but I'm also just like any other girl who happens to also be a soldier. I have no power.

I thank the gods for Pyotr, and hope he finds a way to get that article to Canada! That would be reason enough to stay alive — to see that in print with my name on it.

23.Jan.45
Shlisselburg

I'm so busy, shooting and being shot at all day long. It's hard to find time to write, but it feels important, Yulia. I want to make a record, because who knows, maybe I'll be killed.

They sent me away from the command post (Iah, so shocking I know). "No orders," they said. "Go back to your platoon." I was once again sitting by my lonely fire, so frustrated, when someone joined me.

"Is your name Shanina?" he asked. I didn't answer. "Don't you remember me? I was a friend of Mikhail Panarin."

I looked up, and yes, here was Kolya, Misha's good friend who I'd met a hundred times! It turns out he is head of reconnaissance for the 785th RD, stationed nearby.

He was glad to see me, and asked if I had really received two Orders of Glory. "Almost a Full Cavalier!" he exclaimed, when I said I had. "But why are you here, alone?"

"It's complicated," I said, but he seemed to want more of an explanation. "Everywhere I go, I'm grabbed at and treated to filthy language. I can't stand it, so I leave."

"Ahhh," he looked serious. "Yes, I can see how that could be. Come with me then, and give the 785th a try."

I liked the idea of being near Misha's friend, and went with him, hopefully. These guys were great! What a pleasant surprise to be treated as I used to be, as a comrade, rather than as an object for obscene desires. I thought I'd finally found my home at the Front, but no such luck. The head of the regiment himself started chasing me around, grabbing at me like he was in a brothel. I did nothing to encourage him, and everything to stay away! In the end, I couldn't stand the man and left after just two days. The harassment got worse every minute — I had to leave, and sadly, because the recon guys were so good. *There are bad seeds in every lot*, Mama would say.

During those two days, there were fierce battles. We needed to run lines to the house that we took, past trenches full of heavily fortified German infantry. Our trench system passed by theirs and ended at the estate 150–200 meters away from the house, and they fired on us every time we reached the end of the trench. It was a real meat grinder. Lots of life lost. We ended up putting the troops on top of the self-propelled guns and charged the trench, trying to take out the infantry or get past them that way. It took a lot of tries, and there was just space for one or two troops to have cover and ride safely, everyone else was mowed down. I went into a self-propelled gun to cross, but could not manage to fire my rifle, as I could not look out the hatch without being wounded or killed. When I had crossed, I crawled out and got low, and fired on the Fritz who fled the trench as it was being shelled. Got quite a few that way.

By yesterday night, we had cleaned out the trench and debilitated the anti-tank ditch. I wanted to go on to the house, but the infantry was lying down, afraid to go further. Two *shtrafbat* scouts were going ahead, so I went with them. As a result, the three of us were the first to occupy the estate.

When the infantry saw that we were clear, everyone went on the attack, the infantry and the *shtrafbat*, and we began driving at the heels of the retreating Fritz, like a willow whip snapping at their behinds. I shot as many as I could, and heard later that the commander of the 63rd RD, who were our neighbors on the field, saw me go ahead of the infantry and shouted to his soldiers "Here is this girl's example, learn from it!" Soldiers were running, war cries everywhere, and I heard a shout "Halt!" to my left, and out of the bushes stood two Fritz with their hands up, four meters from me—so close! An icy chill shot through me, as if the Grim Reaper was brushing past.

The action was hot, dangerous, and the scouts were good to me. They sheltered me, saying "You will go with us." We lost fourteen scouts in that one battle. But the Germans were retreating without looking back, and we followed, pushing on towards Germany.

Suddenly we heard a Willys; the driver informed us we were ordered to go back Shlisselburg, the town that was serving as camp. A ZIS soon followed, and picked us up and took us here, where the Germans have ditched everything, cows and all, and fled. Our boys shelled the village. There were frau left behind, and some of the guys dragged them into the woods, to rape, then kill. I don't mean to shock you, Yulia, I'm just being honest.

I can't care about the frau, but I loathe this savage behavior, no matter how many times I see it. So ugly! It might have started with the frau, but now it's everything, everywhere.

24.Jan.1945
Shlisselburg

I think the entire Third Front has moved into camp, and it's impressive, but also so chaotic! We have a huge amount of equipment, and nobody follows traffic rules.

The big iron bridge over the river reminds me of Lermontov, and my eyes keep going to it. We downed trees next to it to serve as an abatis—no time to do it properly. The road is very good, and overlooks the meadow, which is useful. I went into a luxurious house; stone, piano, silk curtains, all of the trappings of a rich German home that we have seen in so many places. Really astonishing that they should wage war because they're not content with what they have. I thought I might steal a corner of some parlor in this elegant home to curl up for the night, but I was kicked out. "Officers only." God knows I have no desire to fall asleep in a house full of officers, so it's all theirs.

The scouts haven't caught up to me yet, busy with work at the edge of the village, so I couldn't count on their help with finding a place to sleep. I'm on my own again, by my little fire, where I now sit, writing you, my dear sister. I have just dashed out what came to mind, because I'm too tired to write carefully. Only getting down the bare bones—I'll add more later.

25.Jan.45

I seem to be doomed to spend the nights under the open sky, in the freezing cold. But the truth is that wherever I try to sleep, someone grabs at me and tries to force me into bed. We've gone back to caveman times, Yulia, where everyone acts on instinct alone, with no respect for civilized behavior. I wouldn't be surprised if someone grabbed me by the hair to pull me across the ice to their cave. Yes, this is war and all that, but it didn't used to be like this. It's partly the chaos and darkness of this place, of Germany.

It was Vadim, son of the chief Colonel, who caused my latest trouble. Last night, I went to the big house in Shlisselburg, and he was drunk. He immediately fell onto me, stuck close, saying "Give me a kiss." I got away from him and went into a parlor to change, closing the door behind me. I was changing, had just taken off my pants, when he burst through the door.

"Get out!" I cried, scrambling for my clothes. He threw himself at me and grabbed my arms, twisting them behind me. He pushed me onto the sofa and started covering me with kisses, putting his hands all over me. I struggled to get free, but he was strong, although small.

Just then his father, the Colonel General, walked in, shouting "What's going on here?"

Vadim stood right away, and said "We're just having some fun, Papa."

"Fun!" I cried, struggling to my feet. "You have a strange idea of fun."

The colonel saw that I was crying, and yelled at his son. "Leave her be, what are you about?"

The colonel apologized to me, with the excuse that the "boys are riled up," and shook his finger at this son.

The evil son lieutenant deflated, said — "All right, all right!" His father left, and he turned on me like this was all my fault, like I was being unreasonable. "Don't you understand," he said, "I don't want German girls. They're dirty, infected. You are a nice, clean Russian girl, and that's what I want."

He looked at me expectantly, like he had paid me a great compliment.

"Don't you understand," I said, in a low, furious voice, "that I don't care what you want. You are not entitled to do as you please with me, simply because you are a boy and I'm a girl."

He looked at me strangely. "But I'm fighting for the Motherland," he exclaimed.

"And what am I doing, milking a cow?" I shouted. Good God. Did this boy not realize that he wasn't the center of the universe?

I forced him to leave so I could finish changing, and I hope he learned something, that evil boy. But I won't count on it.

I knew better than to enter that house full of officers, but I was so cold, Yulia! I ended up sleeping under the stars anyway, the night clear and freezing, and if I was cold, at least I wasn't harassed. This morning, the whole army marched, I with them. We marched all day, and it was good to be warm. Now I sit by yet another fire, but not a lonely one; there are many troops here. Soon it will be dawn. Our task is to push the Germans back into Königsberg and keep them there, isolated. We're making great progress, pushing far into German territory. The Second Front, led by Zhukov, drives west toward the border with Old Germany, and the First Front drives west on the southern end. Everyone moves, herding the fascist beast.

I'm still without papers or orders, and have no real job, but it doesn't seem to matter anymore—the rules no longer exist. My priority is to be useful. I've been doing good sniper work, and everyone accepts me, perhaps because they recognize me from the papers and think I'm a notable sniper. I'm always begging for favors, leaping into battles unasked. But I do good work with my rifle, and everyone knows it. With no boss, no one can tell me what to do, and

I like that, but orders would also be good. Every morning I wake up and wonder—where to go? What to do? What will today bring?

I can't say that I'm happy, Yulia, but I feel like myself, I feel real, and alive. All of the paths and turns I've taken have led me here, to this dark and terrible place, and this is where I belong. I don't need anyone, except for you, and the memories of Misha and Fyodor. You'll have a better life than me, Yulia. This war will be over soon, and new opportunities will open up for you. That makes me happy.

Must close my eyes now, and sleep while I can.

27.Jan.45
Inside an artillery cannon, east of Königsberg

I went with the guns today, pushing north, at the very front of the line, riding inside an artillery cannon like I used to do with Misha, but today we encountered resistance, unexpected and fierce. The other two guys in my gun team have been killed, and I'm trying to find some sign of life from the other guns, but I can't see anything. Something hit me on the side of my head, and I've bandaged it. I think it's not too bad—I'm just a little dizzy. The situation is serious, Yulia, and I don't know what to do. Should I leave the gun and look for another unit, or had I better stay here and wait for reinforcements? The radio is destroyed, so I can't expect help there. I have some water but no food. I'll be fine for a little while, but I'm very cold, very sleepy. And everything inside the gun is covered in blood, including me. If I look closely, I'll vomit. How on earth will I be able to sit here and wait for someone to save me? No one is likely to come soon, with the Fritz resistance so strong, but if I leave the gun now, I'm sure to be shot. They're out there, and I'm alone. But you are with me, Yulia. And I'm still alive.

How amazing, the human body. That my brain forms thoughts, translates them into symbols, that my hand moves to transfer these thoughts onto paper. I've never been so aware, so alive. My fingers are a miracle. My eyes—what an astonishing thing, to see the world and translate it into so many layers of meaning, from a moment's vision. I feel my lungs expanding with air, and expelling stale breath. I feel the blood flowing through every part of my body. How much I've taken for granted! How little I've appreciated the enormity of human life. Even now, when my life has become so loathsome, I want more of it. I want to relish it.

If only I could start over again, and be a baby on the *Bogdanoskoya* farm. Go through the whole thing again… God, no, I don't want that. What could I do differently, if I had a second chance? There's nothing. I've done my best, with what I've been given. There are things I could do better, if I had my life to live over, but the essentials would be the same. I don't have many regrets, and I have earned some glory, some admiration. I'm not ashamed of myself, Yulia, and that's something. Perhaps I can accept it. That it's my time to die.

Misha and Fedya have gone ahead, and Lida. And so many others. But I'm scared, Yulia. I'm afraid to die. I, who pride myself on courage, am terrified of being nothing, of ceasing to exist. Will I be there to know what it's like? Maybe there is a God and an afterlife, but what would that be like for me? Would I be tortured forever in Hell for all those men I shot down in cold blood? Or would I be welcomed into Heaven with open arms, as a savior for my people? Or will I end when the breath goes out of my body, and become another corpse for the pile?

I have often thought of that day in Bereznik when you and I watched that prize hog get slaughtered, by Aunt Agnes' house. We were young, but I think you must remember. It was visceral and commonplace and horrible all at once. I don't know the name of the man who killed the pig, although we must have seen him a hundred times, but the pig was called Whiskers. He was an old hog, and he didn't have a bad life, wandering around the pen with plenty to eat, harassing the sows and doing just as he pleased. But it was his time to go, and we felt very sorry for him. You turned away as he was stabbed in the neck, but I watched the life drain from his eyes. Neither of us ate any part of Whiskers, feeling that he shouldn't have had to give up his life for us to have food. Remember? We were so young.

Lying here on this cold metal bench, with a scarf wrapped around my bleeding head, and the bloody corpses of two good guys for company, I keep imagining myself as Whiskers, hanging by his hooves, except with an awareness that he happily lacked. That might sound resentful, but I don't feel that way. I'm just very aware of myself, aware that my life has been a series of sacrifices to feed other people's lives. When I joined the army, I was willing to give my life for the happiness of others, and the feeling has only grown. I'm okay with it, truly, especially if I think that my life has helped you and our little brothers, has made things safer for you, more pleasant, more just. Perhaps we all live to feed the lives of those who come after us — to fuel a better humanity.

The critic in my head sneers at me, asks "What have you done?" Maybe it's not as much as some, but I've done what I could. I think I have helped, but was it enough?

When will it be enough? Misha asked, that afternoon by the Nemen.

I leaned in close, whispered — *Never*.

Oh, to have those moments back, when we would flirt with a solemn subject and turn it on its head! Misha taught me how to do that. How to toss words up in the air and change their meaning — change them into something to ease the burden, rather than make it heavier. If only there was a way to put words together to change my current situation. But somehow that's attached to Misha, and he's not here. God, how I miss him.

I wanted to live an extraordinary life, but what hope do any of us have at standing out in an important way? How can one person make a difference in the trajectory of human existence? It doesn't often happen, Yulia. But together, as a group, we matter, we *can* make a difference. And we have, in this war. In this world.

I must have dozed off, and woke up in the death scene of the gun's interior. It wasn't easy, but I've pried my way out and started a small fire, which I'm not sure was a good idea, but it's hidden by the cannons, more or less, and I need the warmth.

Misha visited me while I slept. He came to me in a dream. We were in the woods near Yedma on a warm, sunny day, and I was standing in a green meadow, very green, full of purple and yellow flowers. Everything sparkled in the sun, and there was a charge in the air. Even the flowers seemed to crackle with excitement. I saw Misha down the slope by the stream in the valley, looking at me, waiting for me. He was smiling, and I was so happy to see him.

"Misha!" I called, but he didn't answer, and didn't come toward me. He stood still by the stream, looking at me, beaming, I ran down the slope to him, and he held his arms open. I fell into them, and he wrapped himself around me, strong, gentle, and hugged me tight. I hugged him back, so solid and familiar, and all my darkness disappeared.

The sky was a brilliant orange and yellow, and I knew that it touched everything, even the parts of the world we could not see. Then somehow we were part of the sky, looking down from above. A sea was on the horizon, and I felt something rise out from it—a female presence. She seemed to reach her arms out and hold everything close to her, not in a stranglehold, more of a loose hold, but she wasn't going to let one ray of light escape. She was a loving presence, all-powerful, holding everything in her arms, but she had no body, nothing that could be seen. I thought she was the Earth Mother, Yulia. And as she spread herself out to touch everything, the light and warmth increased, and I knew that she had done that. I closed my eyes and felt the love and peace she was offering. Somehow, I knew she was smiling at me, looking at me specifically and pushing her smile into me.

Everything is as it should be, she said, without words, and I felt the truth of it wash over me, along with a powerful calmness. I felt truly safe, and adored. I think she was showing me eternity, Yulia, and it was so beautiful, so loving. Something bigger, beyond our universe, of which I was a precious part. No war, no cold or hunger, just peace and warmth forever and ever.

I woke up knowing that we're part of something bigger and more beautiful than I've ever suspected, and that the *istina* truth is the one that matters, after all. Maybe in life, what we think is true has more power, but what are the petty concerns of life next to all of eternity? Gravel. Life and death—just rocks on the horizon.

I may die here in this field, but I'm not afraid. I'm not sad. I can't remember ever being this calm, this grateful. Whenever I do die, I'll be with Misha, and Fedya, and Lida. And we will have peace! That peaceful eternity that the Earth Mother showed me. One day, we will all have that, Yulia. I love you so much, sister! I'm sorry to leave you, but you'll be fine. We'll all be fine.

AFTERWORD

Roza Yegorevna Shanina was mortally wounded in combat action on 27 January, 1945, just outside of Königsberg, Germany, close to where she made her last journal entry. Senior Sergeant Nikolai Lyantsev and another soldier heard a woman screaming, and upon running to help, found Roza lying on the ground, her chest and abdomen sliced open by a shell fragment, screaming "Shoot me." They did not do as she asked, instead they bandaged her up and carried her to the field hospital, where she died the next day. She was twenty years old.

The hospital staff attempted to give Roza a nice burial, under a tree on the bank of the Alle River, and someone played Chopin's "Funeral March" on the piano as they carried her out of the hospital. In 1947, her ashes were moved to their current resting spot, a private grave in the Mass Grave of Soviet Soldiers, Znamensk, Kaliningrad Oblast.

Marat Shanin, Roza's youngest brother, remembers their mother's words upon hearing of Roza's death: "Maybe it's for the best that she's died. Otherwise, how would she have been able to live after the war? She shot so many people."

Sergei Shanin died that same week, although his family didn't receive the death notification until twenty years later. Sergei's guilt was in question, but he confessed to his crimes, and his sentence was changed from hard labor to death by execution and confiscation of property. Sergei was shot by a Soviet bullet on 3 February, 1945.

Aleksandra (Sasha) Ekimova was killed in action on 6 February, 1945, when Germans jumped into a trench where she was working and slit her throat. Kali had stayed home that day, due to illness. Sasha's husband, Vovka, joined her in death a few weeks later.

Kaleriya (Kali) Petrova fought in the Battle for Königsberg, and finished out the war on the Japanese Front. After the war, Kali studied Hydrology at university and went on to become a successful professor at the University of Moscow, as well as a wife, mother and grandmother. Kaleriya Petrova passed away in 2014.

Posthumously, Roza was honored in several ways. The Roza Shanina museum was erected in Yedma, and plaques were placed at schools she had attended. Streets in Arkhangelsk, Shangaly and Stroyevskoye were named after her. In several locations around northern Russia, shooting and sporting competitions boast the Roza Shanina Prize.

Roza's brothers who had been killed early in the war, Fyodor and Mikhail, were both immortalized on a war monument in Yedma. Fyodor's body was never found, and the circumstances of his death are still unknown. Brother Pavel survived his tour of duty, and little Marat and Yulia also survived the war, living in Yedma. After Roza died, the Shanin family moved to Solista, where Yegor Shanin had taken on the role of Party Organizer of the Arkhangelsk Regional Committee of the Communist Party. Two years later, Anna, Yulia and Marat moved to Krasnoyarsk to be with Pavel, who had relocated there after the war.

Roza's mother, Anna Alexeyevna, died in Krasnoyarsk in 1964 at 73 years old. Her father, Yegor Mikhailovich, followed Anna in death four years later, bitterly complaining about the de-Stalinization of the Soviet Union to the end. Yulia, Marat and Pavel lived long, full lives, for which they credited their fallen siblings who "died so they could be free."

After Roza's death, the Third Belorussian Front continued to push toward the German city of Königsberg, losing many troops to fierce German resistance. Although the Germans were clearly on the run, they staged an impressive last-ditch effort to defend their territory, and the clash culminated in the four-day long bloody battle for Königsberg on 5 April, 1945, when the Soviets emerged victorious and took over the city, a key stronghold for the Nazi regime.

Further south, the Second Belorussian Front pushed hard and fast westward over the German mainland, meeting up with the First Belorussian Front just shy of Berlin. United, the two massive fronts, comprised of 1.5 million Soviet soldiers, overtook Berlin on 25 April, 1945, causing as much death and destruction to that city's citizens as the German army had wrought upon them four years earlier during their "Operation Barbarossa"—the invasion of the Soviet Union.

Hitler committed suicide the following day, on 26 April, 1945.

2,484 Soviet women served as snipers during World War Two, around 500 survived. They were collectively responsible for more than 12,000 confirmed kills. An estimated 24,000,000 Soviet soldiers and citizens died during World War Two. They are still finding bodies along the Eastern Front. Germany lost as many as 8,800,000, Japan lost up to 3,000,000, while the United States lost 418,500, the United Kingdom 450,700. The People's Army of the Soviet Union cut out their own hearts and carried them into battle in their fists, held high in the air, whooping their war cry. That they came to war from a hard place cannot be doubted, but whatever their hardships, whatever their politics, they were united in a strong, warrior spirit that turned the tides of World War Two toward the allies.

A NOTE FROM THE AUTHOR

The Soviet Union is remembered famously for recreating history and blurring the line between truth and fiction. Researching and writing *Roza's War* was a four-year-long labor of love that involved a lot of investigation into a subject that is pretty difficult to investigate—an individual's life in Soviet Russia. Fortunately, I was able to root out enough information about Roza Shanina to form a backbone of historical fact to support my narrative. While *Roza's War* is a work of fiction, it is built around real people and real events, and for those who want to know more about that, I shall explain.

The basic story of Roza's life is quite real, and to the best of my knowledge, Roza's actual location in time as depicted in the text and maps are accurate—both her progress on the front lines and her movements during early life. The dates are nearly accurate. Her backstory from age eight up until her deployment is well documented, as are some of her relationships with family members—her difficult relationship with father Yegor, her closeness to brother Fyodor, and her fondness for Yulia, her little sister.

In truth, we don't know where Roza was born. The only hint we have as to where she spent the first eight years of life is a blog stating that her father was head of the "Bogdanovka" communal farm during that time. Sadly, nothing remotely resembling "Bogdanovka" appears in the official list of Soviet *kohlkozi* in 1924–1932, but after a considerable amount of research I found a similarly-named farm in Eastern Ukraine, and knowing that the Shanins "fled to Yedma" in 1932 when the farm failed, I came to the conclusion that they might very well have been fleeing the *Holodomor* when it was at its peak. It seems the most plausible scenario.

Barring the above assumption, the Preface is historically accurate, with a fictional addition at the end that refers to Yulia having given Roza her first journal. In truth, we have no way of knowing what items Roza had in her possession when she deployed, much less from where or whom she would have gotten them. The Afterword is factual, while the journal itself is a work of fiction, in which all scenes and characters are products of my imagination.

Keeping a journal was against Red Army rules during the Great Patriotic War, but Roza kept one anyway. Three separate volumes of her journal survived and are on display in Arkhangelsk at the Regional Museum of Arkhangelsk Oblast. An English translation is available at rozasdiary.com. Roza's fellow snipers have said that Roza wrote in a journal throughout her entire tour of duty, but the earliest date in the surviving volumes is October 6, 1944.

Roza's voice and character was channeled into my imagination via the English translation of her surviving combat journals, research into her life story, and an understanding of the conditions of life in the Soviet Union during her time. I like to think I got her right, but the end result may or may not depict who she really was as a living person.

We know that Roza's eldest brother, Sergei Shanin, was quite a bit older than her. He was in his thirties during the war, married with children, based out of Moscow. I have the impression that Roza didn't know him well, and wonder if he was the child of a different mother, since Roza had much younger siblings birthed by her own mother. Sergei's presence in the book grew out of a comment Roza made in her diary when she found out that Sergei had been arrested and thrown in prison. The official report states that Sergei Shanin hung himself in prison in Febuary of 1945, but there are reports of him having been executed Soviet style, *i.e.*, shot in the head. With the frequent falsification of records, it's not possible to know the truth, but it's likely that Sergei was shot by the

NKVD. Within the context of *Roza's War*, Sergei's characteristics, personality and storyline are entirely imaginary, based on the above known facts.

Mikhail and Fyodor Shanin, Roza's older brothers, were both killed in combat but their bodies were not recovered. Fyodor's death notice came more than a year after he stopped sending letters. Recovering bodies became such a problem for the USSR that they devised a system to avoid having to do so — they replaced durable dog tags with flimsy plastic bottles containing pieces of paper that identified a soldier's name and rank. These bottles broke easily, and the papers disintegrated. With this new system, the USSR couldn't identify bodies, thus avoiding the need to send notices and backpay to dead soldiers' families.

Yegor Shanin was by all reports a most unpleasant creature, and was referred to as "Yegor the Lame" by at least some of his children. But we know nothing at all about Yulia, Roza's younger sister, except that Roza was fond of her. As far as I can tell, there is no information about her existence at all, and Yulia's character and storyline in the book are entirely fabricated.

Misha Panarin was one of Roza's boyfriends during her tour of duty, seemingly her first and most beloved, and he was killed in action at some undetermined point in time. Misha's character and storyline are entirely fabricated — he's another one that doesn't exist anywhere.

Alexandra (Sasha) Ekimova and Kaleriya (Kali) Petrova were real-life fellow snipers of Roza's and her closest friends at the front lines. Kali has been described and quoted in some modern publications, but little is known about Sasha's nature. Their personalities in *Roza's War* are largely imaginary, and may or may not depict their actual characters.

Pyotr Malchonov was a real journalist for the Fifth Army's "Destroy the Enemy" publication, and Roza developed a friendship with him during the war. For unknown reasons, Pyotr had possession of Roza's surviving combat diaries for many years after her death. Little is known about his true character, and his personality and storyline in *Roza's War* are entirely imaginary.

Roza really was a "poster child," written up in many magazines and newspapers, and she did struggle with her fame. All of the quotes and snippets from articles that appear in the book are real quotes from actual articles that appeared in magazines or newspapers. It seems likely that Stalin would have come across her photograph on the cover of some publication, but there's no indication that he took any notice or interest in her. That part of the story is probably not real, although it could be.

Roza was photographed often with fellow snipers and soldiers, and she mentions others in her journal. Some of these soldiers' names appear in *Roza's War*, and in such cases, the personalities and events surrounding these people are completely imaginary.

With the exception of public figures such as Stalin and Beria, all characters in *Roza's War* that I haven't listed above are a product of my imagination, and any resemblance to real people is accidental.

With the exception of battle scenes, which are fictional recreations of actual battles in which Roza participated, all scenes and events depicted in the novel are a product of my imagination, based on knowing where she was on a given day and what she might have been doing. Many of these scenes sprang from a seed of truth. For example, we know that Roza Shanina once killed a Nazi sniper, and another time brought in three Nazi prisoners, but as no details are available for either event, the scenes were imagined.

While the action described in battle scenes is a product of imagination, battle names, dates, and locations are historically accurate, as are the names and types of weapons and other equipment in use on the Soviet front. My careful maps and text descriptions of army positions at specific times are accurate.

The Katyn Massacre, widely considered a significant historical tragedy, was a series of mass executions conducted by the Soviet's NKVD upon the Polish, in which they killed an estimated 22,000 Polish officers and scientists. Stalin was incredibly distrustful of Poland, who had expressed skepticism about Communism, and set out to weaken them by destroying the Polish military and intelligentsia. One of Roza's earliest missions took place in the town of Kozie Gory, near Katyn Forest, the site of several mass graves from the Katyn Massacre. The combat diary she kept during that time has disappeared, so we don't know what Roza experienced when/if she came upon those mass graves. This part of the narrative sprang from imagining what might have happened.

The depiction of the general atmosphere of front-line life and the habits of the female Soviet snipers is based on extensive research, and while all scenes were imagined, they're probably not far off from how things actually went down.

There are quite a few books and personal accounts that share stories of abuse perpetrated on the female soldiers of the Red Army during WWII, mostly by Soviet officers, and Roza does describe fighting off one or two would-be rapists in her writings. But she almost certainly did not ask Malchonov to write an exposé on the subject, rather she seemed to be simultaneously mad and sad about the situation, but kept quiet and never complained. Roza's apparent acceptance of her powerlessness to effect change is likely closer to how female Soviet soldiers would have reacted at that time, rather than how my fictionalized Roza behaves.

I appreciate the chance to bring this unsung heroine to life for you. If you're interested in reading more about the female Soviet snipers of the Great Patriotic War, check out the attached annotated bibliography.

Fyodor Shanin in his Red Army uniform

(left to right) Roza with Sasha Ekimova and Lidia Vdovina

Great House at Kozie Gory, circa 1940

НАГРАДНОЙ ЛИСТ

1. Фамилия, имя, отчество ШАНИНА РОЗА ГЕОРГИЕВНА
2. Звание ефрейтор 3. Должность, часть снайпер-снайпер 1138 сп 33 с
Представляется к награде ордена "СЛАВЫ ТРЕТЬЕЙ СТЕПЕНИ"
4. Год рождения 1924 5. Национальность Русская
6. Партийность член ВЛКСМ с 1938 г.
7. Участие в гражданской войне, последующих боевых действиях по защите СССР и Отечественной войне в Отечественной войне с 3.4.1944г.
8. Имеет ли ранения и контузии в Отечественной войне ранений не имеет

С какого времени в Красной Армии с августа 1943г.
Каким РВК призван Первомайским РВК г. Архангельск
Чем ранее награждён наград не имеет
Постоянный домашний адрес представляемого к награждению и адрес его семьи

Краткое, конкретное изложение личного боевого подвига или заслуг.

За мужество и стойкость проявленные при выполнении боевой задачи тов. Шанина несмотря на артиллерийский пулемётный огонь противника, настойчиво выслеживала врага и при появлении уничтожала его из своей снайперской винтовки. Таким образом с 3.4.44г. по 11.4.44г. будучи в р-не обороны 2 сб 1138 сп уничтожила 13 солдат противника.

Достойна Правительственной награды ордена " СЛАВЫ ТРЕТЬЕЙ СТЕПЕНИ

КОМАНДИР 1138 СП
ГВ. МАЙОР /ДЕГТЯРЕВ/

" " Апреля 1944г.

Recommendation for Roza to receive Order of Glory, Third Class

Sergei Shanin in his NKVD uniform, 1943

Photo of Roza taken near Vitebsk, later appeared in Frontline Humor

Roza and Dusya (Duce) Fedorovna Krasnoborova, a fellow sniper, 1944

Nikolai Semenovich Solomatin (center) with unknown comrades

The Stray Troika: Kaleriya (Kali) Petrova, Roza Shanina, and Alexandra (Sasha) Ekimova

Roza at camp with Lida, Sasha and some artillery men

Roza showing her rifle to A. Baleyev

Roza and Sasha Ekimova, November 1944

Roza Shanina, November 1944

Roza Shanina, January 1945

Roza Shanina in winter camouflage

Red Army Girl Unseen Terror Of East Prussia

MOSCOW, Sept. 23 — (AP) — Young Rosa Shanina who wears a sergeant's stripes on the tunic of her Red army uniform is the unseen terror of East Prussia.

An official dispatch from the Sezupe river front where Red army troops face German soil reported the girl sergeant killed five Germans in a single day as she crouched in a sniper's hideout.

Since she first trained her rifle on East Prussian targets, the dispatch said, Rosa has killed 15 enemy soldiers and her total for the war now is 46.

Rosa's duty begins each misty dawn when she crawls through a muddy communications trench to a specially camouflaged pit from which she can overlook German territory.

The other morning she waited motionless and silent as a German machine-gunner appeared at the exit of a pill-box made of sandbags and logs.

When he crawled sleepily toward a rear bivouac Rosa fired. One shot toppled him over. Two comrades rushed out to investigate. Rosa got both. Then two more Germans showed themselves. They also were killed.

A Lady Killer

Her mild manner and demure smile belie the fact that pretty Senior Sergt. Roza Shanina is a crack Nazi-killer. A volunteer sniper, the Russian blonde has shot 54 Germans. She has been decorated for bravery.

ABOUT THE AUTHOR

BRENDA ELLIS is an accomplished writer of fiction and non-fiction and a self-taught expert on Soviet times and Russian literature. She has published numerous non-fiction and short story pieces, and her debut novel, *Roza's War*, was released in the summer of 2024.

For the first ten years of her professional career, Brenda experienced success as a high-tech software consultant for Fortune 50 companies. Upon realizing that Corporate America wasn't a good long-term fit for her, Brenda used her understanding of Jungian Psychology to create PersonalityPage.com, a website dedicated to helping people better understand and tolerate each other. The site has reached over 400,000,000 people.

In recent years, Brenda has focused her work efforts toward creating stories set in the Soviet era, where life was fleeting and intense. *Roza's War* recreates the combat journal kept by Soviet sniper Roza Shanina during her tour of duty on the Eastern Front of WW2. Brenda is at work on her second manuscript (working title *The Ghost of Moscow*), a political thriller that takes us on a journey with Roza's brother, Sergei Shanin.

BIBLIOGRAPHY

Alexievich, Svetlana. *"The Unwomanly Face of War: An Oral History of Women in World War II."* Translated by Richard Pevear and Larissa Volokhonsky. New York, Random House, 2017.

Alexievich, winner of the Nobel Prize in Literature, recorded hundreds of personal stories from surviving female Soviet soldiers and nurses, and consolidated them into *"The Unwomanly Face of War."* The resulting manuscript is a beautiful, written collage that provides insight into what it was like for the Soviet women who served during WWII.

Figes, Orlando. *"The Whisperers: Private Life in Stalin's Russia."* New York, Picador, 2007.

Figes' book conveys the struggles of the Soviet people during Stalin's reign as leader of the Soviet Union, with emphasis on the unscrupulous antics of the government and their effect on its citizenry.

Glantz, David M. with Glantz, Mary Elizabeth. *"Battle for Belorussia: The Red Army's Forgotten Campaign of October 1943—April 1944."* Lawrence, Kansas, The University Press of Kansas, 2016.

The Glantz manuscript provides sweeping documentation about the battle for Belorussia, including specific military details about all of the major battles, such as which troops and armies were present, with what weaponry. It also describes the overall feel and direction of the war at every turn during that campaign.

Kotkin, Stephen. *"Stalin: Volume 1—Paradoxes of Power."* New York, Penguin Press, 2014.

Kotkin's book provides an authoritative biography of Stalin covering his entire life in detail, including his early years, his rise to power, his character and machinations during his reign of terror, and his ultimate death.

Litvin, Nikolai. *"800 Days on the Eastern Front: A Russian Soldier Remembers World War II."* Lawrence, Kansas, University Press of Kansas, 2007.

Litvin's journey along the Eastern Front was remarkably similar to Roza Shanina's—they participated in some of the same battles. His memoir depicts Red Army life along the Third Belorussian Front during WWII.

Lugovskaya, Nina. *"The Diary of a Soviet Schoolgirl, 1932–1937."* Moscow, GLAS, 2003. Distributed in the U.S. by Northwestern University Press.

Nina Lugovskaya (sometimes called the "Anne Frank of Moscow") was a precocious teenager who was born around the same time as Roza Shanina. Her diary gives insight into early Soviet school life, and the concerns and interests of a girl born into the first Soviet generation.

Miller, Donald L. *"The Story of World War II."* Simon & Schuster 2011.

Possibly the most authoritative source on all things World War II, this tome is a great source of big picture information about the war.

Mogan, A.G. *"Stalin's Sniper: The War Diary of Roza Shanina."*

Mogin's book is a translation of the last three combat journals kept by Roza Shanina. It also contains an interesting section written by Marat, Roza's younger brother, and copies of two surviving letters that were sent to the Shanin family by Fyodor, Roza's closest older brother.

Pyl'cyn Alexander V. *"Penalty Strike: The Memoirs of a Red Army Penal Company Commander, 1945-45."* Stackpole Books, 2009.

Pylcyn's book paints a picture of life in a WWII Soviet *shtrafbat*, or "suicide squad," comprised of disgraced officers and prisoners.

Rozasdiary.com. "The Frontline Life of Roza Shanina." English translation of the abridged version of Roza Shanina's combat journals that were published in 2011 and 2016 by the Arkhangelsk Regional Museum.

Rozasdiary.com is the best English translation of Roza Shanina's surviving combat journals that I've found, and is an excellent resource for public domain photos relating to Roza. Although Roza's diary entries are quite terse, they convey her frame of mind and the struggles she faced throughout the latter part of her tour of duty.

Solzhenitsyn, Alexandr. *"Apricot Jam: And Other Stories."* New York, Counterpoint Press, 2011.

Apricot Jam is a late-published compilation of short stories and essays by Solzhenitsyn that includes a few vivid, realistic stories about his time on the Eastern Front of WWII.

Vinogradova, Lyuba. *"Avenging Angels: Young Women of the Soviet Union's WWII Sniper Corps."* English translation Copyright Arch Tait, 2017. New York, MacLehose Press, 2017.

Vinogradova's big and rambling reference work is a synthesis of interviews with surviving female Soviet snipers, including Roza's close friend Kaleriya Petrova. It is full of vignettes and moments from the snipers' lives on the Front.

Zaitsev, Vassili. *"Notes of a Russian Sniper."* Translated by David Givens, Peter Kornakov and Konstantin Kornakov, edited by Neil Okrent. London, Frontline Books, 2015. Originally published in German in 2008.

Zaitsev's memoir is primarily a first-hand account of his work as a sniper in the battle for Stalingrad. Zaitsev describes specific battle scenes in detail from his perspective as a sniper.

Zhukova, Yulia. *"Girl with a Sniper Rifle: An Eastern Front Memoir."* London, Greenhill Books, 2019.

Zhukova's memoir covers her life before, during and after her tour of duty as a female Soviet sniper in WWII. Her descriptions about her time spent as a sniper are rich with interesting details about her daily life from sniper school to the front lines.

www.hellgatepress.com

www.ingramcontent.com/pod-product-compliance
Lightning Source LLC
LaVergne TN
LVHW051826080426
835512LV00018B/2740